FIVE-MINUTE WARM-UPS

FOR ELEMENTARY GRADES

REVISED EDITION

Quick-and-Easy Activities
to Reinforce Basic Skills

by Bea Green, Sandi Schlichting, and Mary Ellen Thomas

Incentive Publications, Inc.
Nashville, Tennessee

Special acknowledgment is
accorded to Marjorie Frank
for creating new activities
to be included in this publication.

Cover by Kristy Jones
Edited by Charlotte Bosarge

ISBN 0-86530-625-7

Copyright © 2004 by Incentive Publications, Inc., Nashville, TN. All rights reserved. No part of this publication may be reproduced, stored in a retrieval system, or transmitted in any form or by any means (electronic, mechanical, photo-copying, recording, or otherwise) without written permission from Incentive Publications, Inc., with the exception below.

Pages labeled with the statement ©**2004 by Incentive Publications, Inc., Nashville, TN** are intended for reproduction. Permission is hereby granted to the purchaser of one copy of **FIVE-MINUTE WARM-UPS FOR ELEMENTARY GRADES, REVISED EDITION** to reproduce these pages in sufficient quantities for meeting the purchaser's own classroom needs.

1 2 3 4 5 6 7 8 9 10   07   06   05   04

PRINTED IN THE UNITED STATES OF AMERICA
www.incentivepublications.com

Table of Contents

Introduction 7

MATH

Fractions with Personality (Fractions) 10
Math without Pencils (Mental Math) 10
Sense or Nonsense? (Number Sense) 11
Geometry Look-Out (Geometry) 11
What's the Pattern? (Number Patterns) 12
Take a Chance on Socks (Probability) 12
Who's Where? (Ordinals) 13
Which Worm? (Place Value) 13
Count or Measure? (Measurement) 14
Working Math (Real-Life Situations) 14
Symbol Truth (Symbols) 15
What's Wrong? (Finding Mistakes) 15
Size-Wise (Ordering by Size) 16
Number Actions (Counting) 16
Operations (Problem-Solving) 17
Calling Time (Telling Time) 17
Bonkers, Jr. (Identifying Digits) 18
Turtle Race (Story Problems) 18
Math Line-Up (Knowledge) 19
Math Line-Up II (Knowledge) 19
Twelve Questions (Guessing Numbers) 20

Add or Subtract? (Problem-Solving) 20
Ruler Race (Measuring) 21
Shape Up (Creating Shapes) 21
Place It (Place Value) 22
Race to 25 (Counting Strategy) 22
A Different View (Creative Thinking) 23
Double Digits (Problem-Solving) 23
Ordered Numbers (Ordering Numbers) 24
On Target (Number Strategy) 24
Cents Sense (Problem-Solving) 25
Package Deals (Problem-Solving) 25
Time Flies (Time Awareness) 26
Units, Please (Units of Measure) 26
Greater Than, Less Than (Problem-Solving) 27
Just the Facts (Problem-Solving) 27
Measure It (Measurement) 28
Good Fit (Size Awareness) 28
It's Your Problem (Story Problems) 29
Moving On (Problem-Solving) 29
In Between (Problem-Solving) 30
Skipping Numbers (Counting) 30

SOCIAL STUDIES

Birthday Time Line (Time Sequence) 32
Help! (Community Services) 32
Search the U.S. (Geographic Features) 33
So Many Groups! (Social Groups) 33
Picture Words (Map Skills) 34
Interview Time (Famous Persons) 34
Money Names (Currency) 35
Global Awareness (Globe Skills) 35
Political Money (Money Identification) 36
Where Should You Look? (Geography) 36
Not My Job! (Job Responsibilities) 37
Even Exchange (Money) 37
Dollar Sense (Pricing) 38
City, Country, Continent, or State?
 (Geography) 38
At Your Service (Service Jobs) 39
Needs or Wants? (Economics) 39
Where Would You Go? (Communities) 40
Whose Property? (Public or Private Property) 40
In the Know (Consumer Responsibilities) 41

Design-a-Sign (Community Signs) 41
Economics A-Z (Economics) 42
Spotlight on You (Creative Thinking) 42
Your Choice (Opportunity Cost) 43
Rule or Law? (Rules and Laws) 43
Goods or Services? (Goods and Services) 44
Branded (Advertising) 44
Where Could It Be? (Geography) 45
Value Life (Economics) 45
Thumbs Up, Thumbs Down (Polling) 46
History Mysteries (U.S. History) 46
It's a Tradition! (Cultural Traditions) 47
No Money (Barter) 47
It All Depends (Economics) 48
Flags Have Meaning (Cultural Symbols) 48
History in the News (History) 49
Trace It (Manufacturing) 49
On Line (Manufacturing) 50
Small Steps—Giant Steps
 (Cardinal Directions) 50

LANGUAGE ARTS

Crazy Talk (Idioms) 52	What About Ernie? (Listening) 62
Money Talk (Idioms) 52	Seek and Find (Reference Skills) 63
Say When (Past Tenses) 53	Alphabet Soup (Word Formation) 63
The Inside Story (Textbook Information) 53	Prove It (Facts and Opinions) 64
Think Fast! (Impromptu Speaking) 54	Sharp Senses (Writing) 64
10-Second Synonyms (Synonyms) 54	If I Had . . . (Self-Expression) 65
Stretch-a-Sentence (Sentences) 55	Double Trouble (Coining Words) 65
Grand Slam! (Word Formation) 55	Description Dilemma (Word Play) 66
Syllable Relay (Syllables) 56	Boys and Girls (Communication) 66
Topic Treasures (Topic Selection) 56	Counting Fun (Alliteration) 67
Words That Confuse (Homonyms) 57	All in the Family (Word Formation) 67
Looking Good (Descriptive Language) 57	Scavenger Hunt (Table of Contents) 68
Gossip Chain (Communication) 58	Word Pairs (Associated Words) 68
Big Words Made Easy (Context) 58	Yellow is for Jello? (Categorizing) 69
All About Me (Writing) 59	In the Middle (Dictionary Skills) 69
Finish This! (Analogies) 59	Head of the Line (General Knowledge) 70
Poems in a Minute (Poetry) 60	Uncommonly Good (Creative Thinking) 70
Other Ways to Say It (Word Choice) 60	Wonder-Full (Self-Expression) 71
Webbing Words (Related Words) 61	What Happened? (Cause and Effect) 71
Moody Words (Word Interpretation) 61	Seasonal Search (Word Usage) 72
Fill It Fast! (Word Usage) 62	Mouse, Mice . . . House, Hice? (Irregular Plurals)... 72

SCIENCE

So Many Sciences! (Fields of Science) 74	Words From Outer Space (Space Science) 81
What a Difference! (History of Science) 74	Sensational Science (Senses) 82
Great Discoveries (History of Science) 75	Body Jobs (Body Parts and Processes) 82
Science in Every Room (Science Applications) ... 75	Body Alert (Diseases and Disorders) 83
Looking for Causes (Cause and Effect) 76	Bone Smart (Human Body) 83
What Good are Whiskers? (Form and Function) ... 76	Matter Matters (Properties of Matter) 84
Classy Science (Classification) 77	Matter Changes (Changes in Matter) 84
Pay Attention! (Observation) 77	Will It Float? (Water and Floating) 85
Is It Alive? (Life Characteristics) 78	Know Your "-Ologies!" (Fields of Science) 85
In the Wrong Place (Life Classification) 78	Weather-Watching (Weather Conditions) 86
On the Move (Animal Movement) 79	Which Unit? (Measurement) 86
Home Sweet Home (Habitats) 79	Hurray for Electricity! (Electricity) 87
We Know This! (Oceans) 80	Science and Sirens (Sound) 87
Geo-Talk (Earth Science) 80	Guess What? (General Science) 88
Join the Solar System (Solar System) 81	Where Would You Find It? (General Science)...... 88

BONUS: SELF-AWARENESS ACTIVITIES

Fly Me! (Self-Discovery) 90	Compliment Chain (Social Relationships) 92
Which Side? (Making Choices) 90	Just Like Me (Common Attributes) 93
Hidden Friends (Social Relationships) 91	Shoe Business (Observation) 93
I Can! I Can! (Positive Self-Image) 91	One Minute to Go (Get-Acquainted Activity) 94
Only Me (Self-Image) 92	I Used To Be . . . (Self-Discovery) 94

Index 95

INTRODUCTION

Think about all those times during your school day or school week when there are just five or ten minutes left over before the class must move on to something else. Even with the best of planning, it's not possible to eliminate those extra five-minute periods. These are time periods of an unusual length—too short to start a major activity or lesson, but too long to waste. Such a spell of a time may occur just before lunch, just before recess, while you're waiting to send the class to P.E. or music, or while you're waiting for a class visitor, or maybe there are a few minutes at the start of the class when you aren't quite ready to dive into a long unit, or at the end of the class when you've put everything away.

However, when you do a little calculation, you'll realize that five minutes a day adds up to over fifteen hours during a school year. This is valuable instructional time! **Five-Minute Warm-Ups for Elementary Grades** provides just what you need to use these small patches of time for effective reinforcement of skills and concepts in language, math, science, and social studies.

These warm-ups are more than just ways to fill extra moments. You will find that they spark enthusiasm in students, "warming them up" for the next activity, or leaving them "fired-up" with learning as they exit the class. Many of these warm-ups can be used as lead-ins for a new unit or lesson. Others are meant for sharpening basic skills and facts. Some are simply fun-filled ways to put skills and knowledge to work. Just about all of them can be extended into much longer learning lessons.

The book ends with a bonus section of self-awareness activities. The wise elementary grades teacher knows when the atmosphere of trust in a classroom has reached a level where such activities can be of benefit to the group. At first, students may seem reluctant to participate in self-awareness activities. However, when you present them in a non-coercive way and repeat them regularly, you will probably find that these are the activities students most want to extend beyond the five-minute time period.

Now that you have this treasure of short, useful activities with high student appeal, you need not dread those extra moments in your school day's schedule. Indeed, you will look forward to the lulls when you can delight the students with quick but important warm-ups!

Happy teaching!

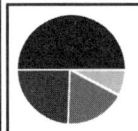
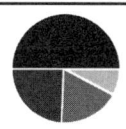

MATH
MATH
MATH
MATH
MATH
MATH
MATH
MATH
MATH
MATH
MATH

MATH

FRACTIONS

FRACTIONS WITH PERSONALITY

Help students actually see how a fraction represents a part of a whole group with human line-ups! Ask students to create their own fractions. You give an instruction such as one of these below. The students' job is to decide how to demonstrate each fraction.

Say to the students: "Form a group in which . . ."

- one-third of the group is wearing a jacket.
- two-sevenths of the heads have hats.
- three-fifths of the group has a name beginning with S.
- seven-twelfths of the eyes are closed.
- five-tenths of the feet are wearing no shoes.
- four-ninths of the group balances on one foot.
- one-half of the group has red noses.

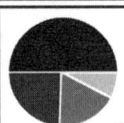

MATH

MENTAL MATH

MATH WITHOUT PENCILS

It's good exercise for the brain to solve problems without writing or seeing the numbers. Give students a few problems such as these. They must listen carefully, and solve the problem in their heads as you read.

- You're at a ball game, and you get hungry. You have $10. You buy a hot dog for $2. You also buy a drink for $1. Later, you get hot chocolate for $1 and popcorn for $1. How much money do you have left?
  (ANSWER: $5.00)

- Your football team scored 6 points in the first quarter, 10 points in the second quarter, 3 points in the third quarter, and 10 points in the fourth quarter. The other team scored 6 points in each quarter. Who won the game?
  (ANSWER: your team—29 to 24)

MATH   NUMBER SENSE

SENSE OR NONSENSE?

One good way to check problem solutions is to ask if they make sense. Some of the answers to real-life problems are reasonable. Others are outrageous—the numbers cannot be right! Read the following number solutions to students. For each one, ask students, "Is this sense or nonsense?"

- The weight of the mosquito was 78 pounds.
- As soon as the soccer game finished, the goalie drank 40 pints of water.
- Granny Lacey served 60 chocolate cookies to her 25 grandchildren.
- Abigail skipped 59 stones across the river in one hour.
- It took the turtle 4 hours to cross the baseball diamond.
- The three friends paid $186.75 for their lunch of hot dogs and lemonade.
- Josie's softball team played 193 games last month.
- Zack's math class estimated that the number of their toes was about 300.

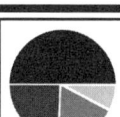

MATH   GEOMETRY

GEOMETRY LOOK-OUT

Take a mental, visual, or actual trip around the classroom or school and look for geometric figures. Make a list of all the real objects you can find in five minutes that are examples of (or contain) these figures:

• square	• cube	• angle
• triangle	• sphere	• right angle
• circle	• pyramid	• acute angle
• rectangle	• cylinder	• obtuse angle
• pentagon	• line	• parallel lines

MATH   NUMBER PATTERNS

WHAT'S THE PATTERN?

Write the following groups of numbers or letters on the board, one at a time. Ask students to examine each group and decide what the pattern is. Once they determine the pattern, ask them to follow the pattern to fill in the missing items.

- 5, 8, 11, 14, 17, _____, 23
  (add 3 to each number; missing: 20)

- 101, 91, 81, 71, _____, _____, _____
  (each number is 10 less;
  missing: 61, 51, 41)

- Z, W, T, Q, _____, K, H, E, B
  (backwards skip 2 letters;
  missing: N)

- A, E, I, M, Q, _____, _____
  (skip 3 letters; missing: U, Y)

- 123, 234, 345, 456, _____
  (consecutive numbers for digits;
  missing: 567)

- 12, 21, 54, 45, 37, 73, 86, _____
  (each two numbers has reversed
  digits; missing: 68)

MATH   PROBABILITY

TAKE A CHANCE ON SOCKS

Get some good practice with probability by bringing an assortment of socks to class. Show students the socks: 6 white, 3 red, 4 black, and 2 blue. Mix the socks up and put them all in a drawer. Tell students that you will choose one sock at a time from the drawer without looking. Ask them questions such as these. Show them how to write chance (probability) as a fraction. (Put the sock back in the drawer each time.)

Say, "I'm going to take one sock out of the drawer."

- "What's the chance that it will be white?" .... (answer: $6/15$ or $2/5$)
- "What's the chance that it will be red?" .... (answer: $3/15$ or $1/5$)
- "What's the chance that it will be blue?" .... (answer: $2/15$)
- "What's the chance that it will be black?" .... (answer: $4/15$)
- "What's the chance it will NOT be white?" .... (answer: $9/15$ or $3/5$)
- "What's the chance it will be black or blue?" .... (answer: $9/15$ or $3/5$)

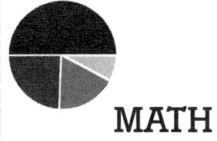

MATH   ORDINALS

WHO'S WHERE?

Randomly choose ten students to line up in front of the door, the teacher's desk, or another designated spot. Use the line-up to sharpen students' skill with ordinals. Ask the rest of the group questions such as the ones below. Then, after a few minutes, form a new group of students.

- Who's seventh in line?
- Where in line is Trisha?
- What color shoes are on the second person?
- Who is next to the eighth person?
- How many girls are between the first and fifth persons?
- Who is fourth in line?
- How do you spell Ramon's place in line?

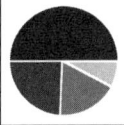

MATH   PLACE VALUE

WHICH WORM?

Draw five fat worms on the board. Label them A-E. Write the following numbers on the worms. Then give students quick place-value practice by asking them questions such as those below.

    A. 3245   B. 6372   C. 8023   D. 1934   E. 5780

- Which worm has the greatest value in the ten's place? (E)
- Which worms have hundreds places greater than 5? (D, E)
- Which worm has a one's place value greater than the other worms? (A)
- Which worm has a thousand's place value twice as great as another worm? (B)
- Which worm has no value in the hundred's place? (C)
- Which worm has the greatest of its digits in the one's place? (A)

MATH MEASUREMENT

COUNT OR MEASURE?

Ask students whether they would count or measure a variety of objects you name. If their answer is "measure," ask them to name the device they would use to do the measuring.

Here is a list of items to start with:
- eggs (count)
- bag of sugar (measure . . . with cup or with scale)
- temperature of water (measure . . . with thermometer)
- length of sidewalk (measure . . . with ruler or meter-stick)
- days in a month (count)
- shoes in the classroom (count)

MATH REAL-LIFE SITUATIONS

WORKING MATH

Students need to be aware that they are learning math facts and skills that they can use in real life, not just in math class. Ask them to decide how math skills (and even which math skills) would be put to work in the following situations:

- You have to share a bag of candy with three friends.
- Mom sends you to the store to buy a loaf of bread.
- You wonder if you have enough money to buy a new toy you see.
- You don't want to miss a special program on TV tonight.
- You are trying to buy a can of soda from a vending machine.
- You want to exchange your bagful of pennies for dimes at the bank.

MATH  SYMBOLS

SYMBOL TRUTH

Write one of these symbols on the chalkboard:

> < =

Have students come to the board and place numbers on either side of the symbol to make a true math statement. Demonstrate with one or two examples to illustrate the idea:

5 = 3 + 2 **5 < 6** **6 > 3**

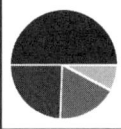 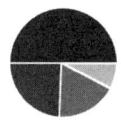

5 Minute Warm-Ups for Elementary Grades, Rev. Ed. ©2004 by Incentive Publications, Inc., Nashville, TN.

MATH FINDING MISTAKES

WHAT'S WRONG?

Write a problem and answer on the board. Make sure that the answer is incorrect. Let students tell what is wrong with the problem. Write answers that would indicate forgetting to borrow, adding instead of subtracting, and so forth.

Another version of this activity would be to put five problems and answers on the board at once. Let students determine which problems have correct answers and which have incorrect answers.

5 Minute Warm-Ups for Elementary Grades, Rev. Ed. ©2004 by Incentive Publications, Inc., Nashville, TN.

 **MATH**   **ORDERING BY SIZE**

SIZE-WISE

Let students practice ordering objects by size with this activity.

Ask them to line up on one side of the room by height, tallest to shortest or shortest to tallest. Or, ask the girls to line up by height on one side of the room. Ask the boys to line up by height on the other side of the room. Then let them merge the two lines into one.

Have students stack their textbooks on top of their desks or tables. The largest book should be on the bottom of the stack and the smallest book should be on top of the stack.

Can they stack their books according to how thick they are?

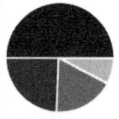 

 **MATH**   **COUNTING**

NUMBER ACTIONS

Let students practice silent counting in a fun way. Select a number between one and seventy-five. Write it on the board or just announce it aloud. Then choose one of the actions below to be performed by the students that many times. Students can be selected individually to perform the action while silently counting the number of times, or the whole class can participate at once. If the action is done by individual students, the rest of the class can determine if the action was done the correct number of times.

Actions to try:
- jumping jacks
- hopping on one leg
- knee bends
- shaking hands with someone nearby
- turning completely around
- hand-clapping
- touching toes
- nodding heads

 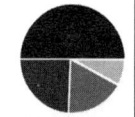

MATH   PROBLEM-SOLVING

OPERATIONS

On the board, list several problems like the ones below. Leave off all signs to identify the operations that complete the problem with the answer given.

Let students go to the board and write signs that correctly complete each problem.

Examples: 10 ___ 5 = 15   2 ___ 1 = 1   14 ___ 3 = 11

```
    15         27         11
   ___7       ___10      ___11
    22         17         22
```

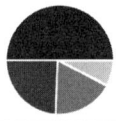

5 Minute Warm-Ups for Elementary Grades, Rev. Ed.   ©2004 by Incentive Publications, Inc., Nashville, TN.

MATH   TELLING TIME

CALLING TIME

If you have a clock face with movable hands, keep it nearby and do this activity at least twice a week for a few minutes.

Hold the clock in front of the class. Set the hands to 12:00. Let the class call out the time in unison. Move the clock hands ahead in increments of 10 or 15 minutes or by half-hours. Students should call out the time each time it is reset. As the students' skill increases, begin to set the minute hand in between the five-minute increments. You may want to let students reset the clock for the rest of the class.

5 Minute Warm-Ups for Elementary Grades, Rev. Ed.   ©2004 by Incentive Publications, Inc., Nashville, TN.

MATH IDENTIFYING DIGITS

BONKERS, JR.

This is an easier version of an intermediate game. Go around the room, letting each student say one number (starting with one). The next student says the number two, and so forth. One rule should be stated first: "If it is your turn, and the next number contains a four (or any other specified digit), you must say 'bonkers' instead of the number." Play continues with the next student.

Example: Teacher: "Don't say any number with a three in it."
First child: "One."
Second child: "Two."
Third child: "Bonkers!"
Fourth child: "Four."
(13, 23, and 30 would be "Bonkers" also.)

MATH STORY PROBLEMS

TURTLE RACE

Quickly divide the class into four teams. Appoint a "turtle" for each team. Line up all the turtles facing a chosen finish line.

Make up a math story problem about turtles and say it aloud. The first team to give the correct answer can have its turtle advance two steps toward the finish line. The team whose turtle reaches the finish line first, or gets closest to the finish line in the playing time, wins.

Examples: Three turtles joined a pond of ten turtles. How many turtles are in the pond now?

Twelve turtles started on a walk together, and six turtles decided to go back to the pond. How many turtles stayed on the walk?

MATH KNOWLEDGE

MATH LINE-UP

When it's time to line up your students to go somewhere, do it in one of these ways:

You may get in line when you can name:
- a multiple of five (or any other number you select)
- a factor of a given number
- a math-related word
- a problem with an answer of ____
- a fraction
- a number greater than ____ (or a number less than ____)

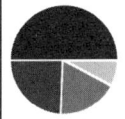 

MATH KNOWLEDGE

MATH LINE-UP II

When it's necessary to have your students line up, let them earn their places in line by naming a number . . .
- . . . with the digit three in it
- . . . that you say when you count by twos
- . . . with digits whose sum is ten

Or by naming something that . . .
- . . . you could measure with a ruler
- . . . is rectangular in shape
- . . . comes in dozens
- . . . has numbers on it (like money)

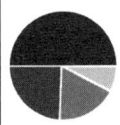 

MATH GUESSING NUMBERS

TWELVE QUESTIONS

Select a number from one to 100. Write it on a slip of paper to hold in your hand. Let students ask questions about your number. Your answers can be only "yes" or "no." Students should try to guess your mystery number in twelve guesses or less.

Good question strategies might include:
- Is it between fifty and 100?
- Is it even or odd?
- Is it a two-digit number?
- Do I say it when I count by fives?

MATH PROBLEM-SOLVING

ADD OR SUBTRACT?

This activity allows students to decide whether addition or subtraction is used to arrive at an answer.

Give a starting number, then give the answer. Students should be able to tell you if you added or subtracted to reach the answer. If you want to have them tell how much was added or subtracted from the original number, that would be even more challenging.

Examples:
- I start with 10. I have 15 for an answer. What did I do? (Added five)
- I start with 12. I have 9 as my answer. What did I do? (Subtracted three)

MATH   MEASURING

RULER RACE

When your students are restless and need to move around, try this measurement activity.

Give students rulers and challenge them to find things in the room that are:
- **almost exactly one foot high, wide, or thick**
- **less than six inches high, wide, or thick**
- **more than nine inches, but less than twelve inches, wide**

Call "time" after two or three minutes of any one challenge and let students share their findings.

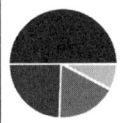

5 Minute Warm-Ups for Elementary Grades, Rev. Ed.   ©2004 by Incentive Publications, Inc., Nashville, TN.

MATH   CREATING SHAPES

SHAPE UP

Give groups of four to six students a long piece of string or yarn (yarn is best). Let the groups spread out around the room. As you call out a shape, the students in each group form that shape with their piece of yarn. Each student in the group should have his or her hands on the yarn, helping to create the desired shape.

Students can form the shapes with the yarn on the floor or in the air.

Try these:

              circle   square   triangle   rectangle   oval

How about having students create the shape of numbers as well?

                   5   2   7   8

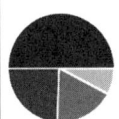
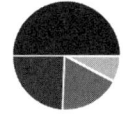

5 Minute Warm-Ups for Elementary Grades, Rev. Ed.   ©2004 by Incentive Publications, Inc., Nashville, TN.

MATH   PLACE VALUE

PLACE IT

This activity gives students some practice in working with place value in three-digit numbers.

Have students draw three blanks in a row on their papers: ___ ___ ___.

As you call out three digits, each student writes each digit wherever he or she wants to on the blanks. Then ask students to share the numbers they made. What was the biggest number possible? What was the smallest number possible? How many possible combinations exist? Share the results.

MATH   COUNTING STRATEGY

RACE TO 25

Students form two teams. The first member of Team A goes to the board and makes the choice to write either "1" or "1" and "2" vertically on the board. The first member of Team B comes to the board and writes either the next consecutive number or the next two consecutive numbers under those already written. The teams continue to send members to the board, adding one or two more consecutive numbers each time. The team whose member writes the number 25 on the board is declared the winner. Play this game several times and watch students begin to develop strategies for winning!

MATH CREATIVE THINKING

A DIFFERENT VIEW

"What else can a number be besides a number?"

Ask your students! Write a digit on the board. Give your class three minutes to name all the things it might be if it were not a number. Encourage creativity and "off the wall" answers.

Example: 3
- a crooked road
- half of an eight
- two toes
- a sideways 'W'

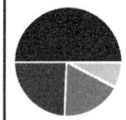

MATH PROBLEM-SOLVING

DOUBLE DIGITS

Write a two-digit number on the board.

Have the students:
- tell the sum of the two digits
- tell the difference between the two digits
- tell the product of the two digits (if they are learning multiplication facts)

Ask the students to write two-digit numbers where:
- the sum of the digits is eight (or any other sum up to 18)
- the difference between the two digits is ___ (any number from 0 to 9)

 MATH ORDERING NUMBERS

ORDERED NUMBERS

After students have learned to write the numbers from one to 100, let them try this activity:

Each student should write a number on a sheet of paper according to the condition set by you. You might ask them to write numbers between twenty and 100. They should write large enough so that everyone can read their numbers when they hold them up.

After everyone has written the numbers, call all or part of the class to the front of the room. Ask them to line up with their numbers in order. If two students have the same number, they should stand next to each other, not in front or back of each other. Let them sit down and call up another part of the class to order their numbers.

 MATH NUMBER STRATEGY

ON TARGET

Have a student name a target number from ten to twenty-five. Other students in the room name numbers of objects that they see. Add the numbers on the board until the target number has been reached. The student that names the last number of items selects the new target number.

Example:
1. Leslie names the number 18.
2. Sue says she sees five blue chairs. Write 5 on the board.
3. Larry says he sees six boys with sneakers on. Add 6 to 5. 11 is the result.
4. Marty says he sees seven girls with hair ribbons. Add 7 to 11.
5. The target number, 18, has been reached.
6. Dionne selects a new target number.

 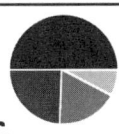

MATH　　　　　　　　　　　　　　　　　　　　　　　PROBLEM-SOLVING

CENTS SENSE

Many students will be able to do the computation mentally. If necessary, let students use scrap paper for this activity.

Ask: "How many cents do I have if I have . . ."

- two dimes
- one quarter
- six nickels
- twelve pennies
- two quarters
- three nickels and one penny
- four dimes and one nickel
- one quarter and one nickel
- five nickels and two pennies
- four quarters and one dime

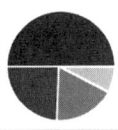 

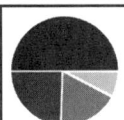 

MATH　　　　　　　　　　　　　　　　　　　　　　　PROBLEM-SOLVING

PACKAGE DEALS

As consumers, your students have to learn to discriminate between real bargain prices and phony bargain prices. Sometimes it is just a matter of knowing which size package to select. A king-size package is not always a king-size bargain.

Ask students which of the following package deals are the better bargains:
- **bubblegum:** 3 for 10 cents or a king-size bag of 5 for 25 cents
- **ice cream bars:** 25 cents each or a king-size bag of 3 for 1 dollar
- **marbles:** small bag of 6 for 15 cents or a king-size bag of 12 for 25 cents.

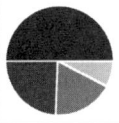 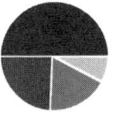

MATH   TIME AWARENESS

TIME FLIES

Young children have difficulty accurately judging the passage of time. This activity lets them practice until they have a "feel" for given periods of time.

Have all students put their heads down on their desks with their eyes closed. Tell them you will say, "Start." Then they are to raise their heads when they think the specified amount of time has passed. Start with fifteen seconds or thirty seconds and work up to three minutes at a time.

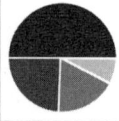 

MATH   UNITS OF MEASURE

UNITS, PLEASE

Make students more aware of standard units of measure by playing these games.
- Name an item and have the students name the standard unit of measure that would be used for that item.
  Examples:
  - flour (pound)
  - gasoline (gallons/liters)
  - fabric or ribbon (yards)
  - canned goods (ounces/grams)

- Form two teams. One team names an item and the other team has to name the appropriate unit of measure. Go back and forth between the teams. Points could be awarded if you want to extend the game.

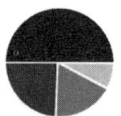 

MATH   PROBLEM-SOLVING

GREATER THAN, LESS THAN

Go around the room quickly, calling on one student at a time. Give each a phrase that describes the number you want him or her to name. The student should respond quickly with a number that meets the condition set forth in the phrase.

Examples:

    Greater than 25   Greater than 12 + 2
    Less than 99   Less than 20 − 5

If you want to increase the difficulty, give two conditions in each phrase (e.g., less than twenty-five and more than three).

MATH   PROBLEM-SOLVING

JUST THE FACTS

Write three to five digits on the board. Choose digits that can be used together to form math facts in addition and subtraction.

Have students call out as many addition or subtraction facts as they can using the digits on the board.

Example:

2, 5, 7	2 + 5 = 7	5 + 2 = 7	7 − 5 = 2	7 − 2 = 5
2, 3, 4, 5, 6	2 + 3 = 5	3 + 2 = 5	2 + 4 = 6	4 + 2 = 6
	6 − 4 = 2	6 − 2 = 4	5 − 3 = 2	5 − 2 = 3

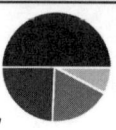

MATH MEASUREMENT

MEASURE IT

Have students measure various things or distances in your room. Instead of using a ruler, have students use a classroom object with which they are familiar as a standard unit.

Some objects to use:
- a new piece of chalk
- the chalkboard eraser
- crayon box

Some distances to measure:
- the width of a desk
- the height of the chair seat
- the distance between desks, windows, etc.

MATH SIZE AWARENESS

GOOD FIT

Being aware of size and comparing items by size are important math skills for elementary students.

- Hold up a shoebox, a cereal box, or other container and ask students to name items that could fit inside it.

- On another day hold up a very small container (a matchbox, a spice bottle, or a small plastic bag). Ask students to name items that could fit in it.

- Ask students to name things that would not fit inside your classroom.

MATH STORY PROBLEMS

IT'S YOUR PROBLEM

Put one of these story problem answers on the board. Call on three different students to invent a story problem to go with it.

Story Problem Answers:
- Six red hens
- Thirteen eggs left over
- Two cents more
- Fourteen dogs in all
- Nine cars remained.
- Then there were seven cats.
- John needed five cents more.
- Only eleven birds were left.

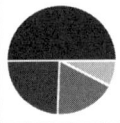

MATH PROBLEM-SOLVING

MOVING ON

Here's a game to practice addition, subtraction, or multiplication problems.

Select one student to start the game. That student stands next to the student in the first seat in the room. The teacher calls out or shows a math problem to both students. The first student to call out the correct answer gets to "Move On" to the next student's desk. (If the standing student wins, he or she moves on. If the seated student wins, he or she exchanges places with the standing student.)

Any student who can make it back to his original starting point can be declared a winner!

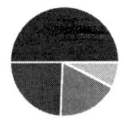

MATH   PROBLEM-SOLVING

IN BETWEEN

Write two numbers on the board. Use numbers that have a difference of at least twenty. Mentally select a number that falls in between the two written numbers. Give your students at least one clue about your mystery number.

Examples:
- It has two digits that are the same.
- It is an odd number.
- You say it when you count by twos.

Let students try to guess your number. Keep track of how many guesses it takes to find the mystery number. Can they improve their guessing strategies on the next game?

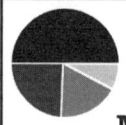

MATH   COUNTING

SKIPPING NUMBERS

Most elementary students learn to count by twos pretty easily. Let students play this skipping numbers game to practice concentration and mental math.

Go around the room. The first student says "one." The next student skips "two" and says "three." The next student skips "four" and says "five." Continue around the room.

Increase the difficulty after using this activity a few times. Let students skip two or three numbers each turn.

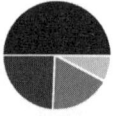

SOCIAL STUDIES
SOCIAL STUDIES
SOCIAL STUDIES
SOCIAL STUDIES
SOCIAL STUDIES
SOCIAL STUDIES
SOCIAL STUDIES
SOCIAL STUDIES
SOCIAL STUDIES
SOCIAL STUDIES
SOCIAL STUDIES

SOCIAL STUDIES   TIME SEQUENCE

BIRTHDAY TIME LINE

Help students grasp the meaning of time sequence and history by focusing on their birthdays and other familiar events in their lives. For this activity, you will need to have a sturdy string or light rope strung across the classroom. You will also need a supply of clothespins and index cards. Give each student a large index card or piece of drawing paper. Ask students to write (in large print) their birthdays, including the year. Then work quickly to hang the birth dates in chronological order. (Include your birth date, too.) If there is time, you might add other familiar events to the time line.

Examples:
- date the school was built
- date of the last presidential election
- date of key events in your neighborhood or city
- dates of key events in the history of the state, country, or world (events happening within students' lifetimes or around the time of their births)

SOCIAL STUDIES   COMMUNITY SERVICES

HELP!

Every community has a wonderful assortment of services available to its citizens. Sometimes we don't stop and think about how much our communities help us.

Here's a way to help students think about what their community has to offer. Ask students to describe the kind of help they could get at each of these businesses or organizations.

- the fire station
- the parks and recreation office
- animal control office
- the police station
- the power company

- the mayor's office
- the garbage collection company
- the division of motor vehicles
- the public library
- the Chamber of Commerce

SOCIAL STUDIES   GEOGRAPHIC FEATURES

SEARCH THE U.S.

Supply a large map of the U.S. to hang in the front of the classroom. Make sure the map shows geographical features. Challenge students to see if they can name at least one example in the United States of each geographical feature below. Ask them to try to give the actual, proper name of the feature.

- an ocean
- a gulf
- a plain
- a swamp
- a lake

- a mountain range
- a river
- an island
- a bay
- a cape

- a canyon
- a delta
- a peninsula
- a peak
- a harbor

SOCIAL STUDIES   SOCIAL GROUPS

SO MANY GROUPS!

Students will be surprised when they discover how many social groups are a part of their lives. Read them the definition of a social group. Point out that a person might be a member of some groups where they don't actually have contact with the other members (e.g., group of Catholics, schoolteachers, or bird watchers). Ask them to name all the social groups that are a part of their lives.

> A **social group** is a number of people who have some interest, purpose, or relationship in common.

Examples:

- school clubs
- a band or orchestra
- a police force
- family
- a choir

- staff at a hospital
- school class
- a sports team
- city bus drivers
- church members

- U.S. senators
- war veterans
- group of friends
- principals in the city
- neighborhood group

33

SOCIAL STUDIES   MAP SKILLS

PICTURE WORDS

Let your students pretend they are making a map of the playground. Give them the following words and let them volunteer to come to the board and draw a symbol of that object, as if it were going to be used on the map legend.

If you have a longer period of time, let each student make a complete set of symbols for a legend on his or her own paper.

Tree	Baseball Diamond	Drinking Fountain
School Building	Restroom	Hot Dog Stand
Slide	Swing Set	Sandbox
Gate	Fence	Bike Rack

SOCIAL STUDIES   FAMOUS PERSONS

INTERVIEW TIME

Let one student name a famous person from the past. Have other students decide what questions they would ask that person if they were doing a newspaper interview with him or her. Make sure that everyone knows why that person is considered famous before you start discussing the interview.

Some suggested persons:

Martha Washington	Amelia Earhart
Betsy Ross	Martin Luther King, Jr.
Paul Revere	John F. Kennedy
Benjamin Franklin	Susan B. Anthony

SOCIAL STUDIES   CURRENCY

MONEY NAMES

Each country has its own currency. See how many of these currencies your students can match with the correct countries. Repeat this activity every couple of weeks and watch their knowledge grow.

Lira	Italy, San Marino, Vatican City	Peso	Argentina, Bolivia, Cuba, Mexico
Yen	Japan		
Franc	Belgium, France	Schilling	Austria, Somalia
Pound	Egypt, Great Britain, Ireland	Dollar	Australia, Canada, Jamaica, USA
Drachma	Greece		
Mark	Germany		

If students are curious about other countries, send them to the library to do some research and let them share their results.

5 Minute Warm-Ups for Elementary Grades, Rev. Ed.   ©2004 by Incentive Publications, Inc., Nashville, TN.

SOCIAL STUDIES   GLOBE SKILLS

GLOBAL AWARENESS

To help students become more familiar with world geography and to give them the opportunity to use globes, try these questions. Allow groups of students to look at globes for three to five minutes while you ask:

- How many countries are in Central America?
- Of which continent is Egypt a part?
- Does the equator pass through South America?
- Is Australia north of any land mass?
- Name some of the largest countries in the world.

Or, allow each student to ask a question of the rest of the class.

5 Minute Warm-Ups for Elementary Grades, Rev. Ed.   ©2004 by Incentive Publications, Inc., Nashville, TN.

SOCIAL STUDIES   MONEY IDENTIFICATION

POLITICAL MONEY

How many of your students can tell you which politician's portrait is on each denomination of currency? Let them try to name them all:

- $1 .... Washington
- $5 .... Lincoln
- $10 .... Hamilton
- $20 .... Jackson
- $50 .... Grant
- $100 .... Franklin

Once students have learned these, ask questions such as:
- How much do I have if I have one Washington and two Lincolns?
- How much do I have if I have one Franklin, two Grants, and a Jackson?
- How much do I have if I have four Hamiltons minus one Lincoln?

5 Minute Warm-Ups for Elementary Grades, Rev. Ed.   ©2004 by Incentive Publications, Inc., Nashville, TN.

SOCIAL STUDIES   GEOGRAPHY

WHERE SHOULD YOU LOOK?

Help students sharpen geography skills by thinking like detectives. Tell students that there are several things in the world for which someone is searching. Ask them to give a quick, general description of where someone should look to find the object or place.

Where would you find . . .

- the Grand Canyon? (western U.S.)
- the world's tallest mountain? (Asia)
- the Panama Canal? (Central America)
- the Sahara Desert? (Africa)
- the Everglades Swamp? (Florida)
- the Great Wall? (China)
- the Mississippi River? (central U.S.)
- the Hawaiian Islands? (Pacific Ocean)
- huge, floating icebergs? (Arctic Ocean or North Atlantic Ocean)
- Antarctica? (south of South America, Africa, Asia, or Australia)
- the Arctic Ocean? (north of Europe or North America)
- the Great Pyramids? (Africa or Egypt or the Middle East)

5 Minute Warm-Ups for Elementary Grades, Rev. Ed.   ©2004 by Incentive Publications, Inc., Nashville, TN.

SOCIAL STUDIES　　　　　　　　　　　　　　　　　　　JOB RESPONSIBILITIES

NOT MY JOB!

Everyone has certain jobs to do. When someone doesn't do his or her job, it creates problems and more work for someone else.

Have students name jobs that are part of family life. List them on the board as they are named. Then discuss what happens when the family member responsible for each job doesn't do his or her part. Who suffers? How is the entire family affected? What should be done about those who don't do their jobs correctly and on time?

Relate the above discussion to career-related responsibilities. How is it the same on the job? How is it different?

SOCIAL STUDIES　　　　　　　　　　　　　　　　　　　　　　　　MONEY

EVEN EXCHANGE

Name an amount of money and tell which bills or coins can be used to make up that amount. Students should name one or more ways to make that same amount using different combinations of bills or coins.

Examples:
- 25 cents (one quarter . . . two dimes and one nickel . . . five nickels)
- $3.10 (three one-dollar bills and one dime . . . twelve quarters and two nickels)
- $10 (one ten-dollar bill . . . one five-dollar bill and five one-dollar bills)

This practice can be extended at an independent center if you have a supply of play bills and coins. Just write different amounts on index cards and let students see how many different ways they can make each amount.

SOCIAL STUDIES   PRICING

DOLLAR SENSE

Kids are often unaware of the actual cost of items that they use all the time. Since they are not usually responsible for the purchase of the items, they seldom pay attention to the prices.

Name a few items that kids use frequently and let them see how close they can come to naming the correct price. Be sure to use items that you know the price of, or have students find out the prices and report back to the class.

You might use:
- current fad toys (popular dolls, video games, etc.)
- cost of a movie ticket
- cost of a pound of meat
- cost of popular brand of athletic shoes
- amount of money spent on classroom supplies per child

5 Minute Warm-Ups for Elementary Grades, Rev. Ed.   ©2004 by Incentive Publications, Inc., Nashville, TN.

SOCIAL STUDIES  GEOGRAPHY

CITY, COUNTRY, CONTINENT, OR STATE?

Prepare for this activity by writing each of the names below (in large print) on an envelope. (You may read the names from the list if you do not have time to prepare envelopes.) Tell students that you have several pieces of mail, each of which needs to be sent to a city, country, continent, or state. Show and read the name on each envelope. Ask students to help you sort them into groups by telling whether the name belongs to a city, country, continent, or state.

- Chicago
- Arizona
- Iraq
- Europe
- San Francisco
- Asia
- Brazil
- Tokyo
- London
- Idaho
- Vermont
- Honolulu
- Belgium
- India
- Spain
- Paris
- Germany
- Australia
- Toronto
- Egypt
- Africa
- Moscow
- Kansas
- Argentina
- Doha

5 Minute Warm-Ups for Elementary Grades, Rev. Ed.   ©2004 by Incentive Publications, Inc., Nashville, TN.

SOCIAL STUDIES   SERVICE JOBS

AT YOUR SERVICE

Even students can provide services. If you were to set up a student service bureau at your school, what could your students do? Ask your class to list as many services as they can. Here's a list to get you started:

- empty trash cans
- file papers
- clean desks, chalkboards
- tutor younger students
- care for classroom pets

- shelve library books
- show visitors around
- deliver messages
- put up bulletin boards
- make morning announcements

SOCIAL STUDIES   ECONOMICS

NEEDS OR WANTS?

Help students distinguish between needs and wants. Name the items below, one at a time. Let students respond with "need" or "want."

- shoes
- computer
- television
- prescription drug
- candy bar
- video game
- home/shelter
- textbook
- newspaper

Be sure to allow discussion of any item upon which students do not agree. Make a "needs" and "wants" bulletin board. Encourage students to add items to it.

SOCIAL STUDIES   COMMUNITIES

WHERE WOULD YOU GO?

The local community supplies many of the needs of daily life. Because parents take children so many places, or buy most of the things the family needs, children often don't stop to think about how much the community provides for them. Ask these questions to get them thinking about the resources in their communities. Some of the questions can have several answers.

Where would you go to . . .

- get a good book?
- eat a pizza?
- get advice about how to treat a bee sting?
- rent a movie?
- learn something new?
- practice batting a softball?

- recycle soda pop cans?
- save some money?
- buy a dog collar?
- get stitches in a split lip?
- get some exercise?
- get rid of old newspapers?

5 Minute Warm-Ups for Elementary Grades, Rev. Ed.   ©2004 by Incentive Publications, Inc., Nashville, TN.

SOCIAL STUDIES   PUBLIC OR PRIVATE PROPERTY

WHOSE PROPERTY?

Review the definitions of public and private property.

Private Property: property owned by individuals or groups of individuals
Public Property: property owned by all the people for everyone's use

Read the items on the following list and let your students respond with "public" or "private."

Yellowstone National Park	Statue of Liberty
Little League Ball Park	Community Swimming Pool
Sears Stores	Jones Brothers' BMX Bike Track
School Playground	K-Mart Stores

5 Minute Warm-Ups for Elementary Grades, Rev. Ed.   ©2004 by Incentive Publications, Inc., Nashville, TN.

SOCIAL STUDIES CONSUMER RESPONSIBILITIES

IN THE KNOW

Being a wise consumer means being a responsible consumer. One important responsibility of a good consumer is knowing what questions to ask about products that are being considered for purchase.

Have students decide what to ask and what to look for as they consider purchasing these items:

- New bicycle: Does it come assembled? What kind of guarantee is there? Where do I buy parts for it? Is it the right size for me?
- Home computer: Are there instruction manuals with it? Does everything I need come with it? Will it do more than play games? How can I get service for it? Is the price competitive with similar computers?
- A pair of jeans: How well are they made? Do they require special cleaning care? Do they fit really well? Will they shrink? Are they too "faddish?" Are they worth the price being asked?

SOCIAL STUDIES COMMUNITY SIGNS

DESIGN-A-SIGN

Get students thinking about how signs communicate important information by letting them design their own signs. Signs don't talk, but they do tell all kinds of important things. There are many signs around any community giving necessary messages. Divide students into teams of two. Give each pair a paper in the shape of a large circle, rectangle, hexagon, or triangle (or, let students decide the shape of the sign themselves). Assign each pair one of these "messages." Ask them to design a sign that communicates the message to anyone who looks at the sign. Examples:

- school crossing
- poison
- steep stairs
- no littering
- telephone
- no smoking
- wash your hands
- no loud noises
- beware of the animal
- restrooms
- quiet
- dangerous water
- electric fence
- fast-moving traffic
- children playing

SOCIAL STUDIES   ECONOMICS

ECONOMICS A–Z

Choose one of the following ideas, and let students name items for every letter of the alphabet.

- products that you could survive without
- products that are advertised on television
- items worth about one dollar
- products you could not survive without
- services offered in your community
- products that might not be around in ten years

SOCIAL STUDIES   CREATIVE THINKING

SPOTLIGHT ON YOU

Role playing is an easy way for students to formulate ideas. Tell them to put themselves in these situations. Call on various students to do the role playing.

- You are a forest ranger. What should you tell people about the importance of preserving our forests?
- You are a foreign child visiting the United States. What do you want to find out about this place?
- You are living in the year 2075. Tell about the sources of energy that you use.
- You are living on a small island. A ship with 5000 people lands on your island and all 5000 decide to stay. How do you feel?

SOCIAL STUDIES   OPPORTUNITY COST

YOUR CHOICE

People have to make choices about how to spend their time and how to spend their money. When you give up something for something else, the thing you give up is called the "opportunity cost" of the item you chose.

Let students practice making choices and recognizing the opportunity costs of those choices by responding to these questions.

- You have $25. You need a new shirt for the PTA play, and you need a new tire for your bike. Which do you choose? What is the opportunity cost?
- You are invited to a friend's birthday party on the same day that your brother is playing in the championship ball game. Where will you go? What will be your opportunity cost?

SOCIAL STUDIES   RULES AND LAWS

RULE OR LAW?

Read the description of a rule and a law. Discuss the differences with students. Then examine each statement, sign, or phrase below. Let students decide if it is a rule or a law.

A **rule** is a statement about how people in a group should behave.

A **law** is a rule for a large group or community, usually made and enforced by a government agency.

- Don't push in line.
- Speed Limit: 55 M.P.H.
- Make your bed every day.
- Stop at red lights.
- Quiet in the library!
- Private Property: No Trespassing
- Do not throw food in the lunchroom.
- $250 fine for littering on state highways
- No gum-chewing in this class!
- No shoplifting!

SOCIAL STUDIES   GOODS AND SERVICES

GOODS OR SERVICES?

Discuss briefly the definitions of goods and services.

Goods: things you can touch which are made by humans.

Services: work done by people which usually does not produce things you can touch (teaching, mowing grass)

Let each student who wants to participate tell what his or her parents (or guardians) do for a living. The rest of the class should decide whether the parents (guardians) provide goods or services. If there is disagreement, refer to the definitions above.

SOCIAL STUDIES   ADVERTISING

BRANDED

Advertisers want you to remember their products. How effective are they at "branding" their item?

See how many brands students can recall for the following items.

ketchup	fast food places
paper towels	airlines
soft drinks	service stations
breakfast cereals	department stores
types of gum	snack foods
pain relievers	grocery stores

SOCIAL STUDIES   GEOGRAPHY

WHERE COULD IT BE?

Increase student familiarity with the general locations of countries and continents by playing this game. Display a current, large world map with political divisions. Ask a student to choose (silently) a country or general location in the world where someone might live. Then the student must tell out loud a general description of the home's location. A second student will come to the world map and point out a possible area where the home could be.

Examples:
- Lucas lives in a home on the shore of the India Ocean. Where could it be?
- Gigi's home is on the equator in Africa. Where could it be?
- Bonita's home is on the west coast of Canada. Where could it be?
- Ivan's home country is next to France. Where could it be?
- Ungu's island is in the Pacific Ocean north of the equator. Where could it be?

SOCIAL STUDIES   ECONOMICS

VALUE LIFE

Some things that we purchase have a long life span. Other things are consumed or discarded shortly after they are purchased. Have students name items that are:

- used only once then discarded (first-aid strips, straws, napkins)
- used completely in one use (food, drinks, gasoline, medicines)
- used more than once but last less than a year (pencil, soap, some shoes and clothes)
- last longer than a year, but are eventually discarded (clothes, automobile tires, electrical appliances)
- last "forever" (house, driveway, swimming pool)

SOCIAL STUDIES   POLLING

THUMBS UP, THUMBS DOWN

Read these statements to your students. Have them show "thumbs up" if they agree with the statement and "thumbs down" if they disagree with the statement.

- Everyone should dress alike.
- Corn is the best vegetable.
- You should be allowed to choose your own bedtime.
- Teachers don't understand kids.
- It is unfair for some people to have more money than others.
- Parents who spank their children are cruel.
- Everyone should learn to like broccoli.
- School should be year-round, not just ten months a year.

SOCIAL STUDIES   U.S. HISTORY

HISTORY MYSTERIES

Ask students to use their knowledge of history and their good sense to solve some history mysteries. Read each question and group of answers. See how many they can answer correctly.

- Which came first?
  U.S. became a country.
  Columbus discovered the Americas.
  Gold was discovered in California.
- Which came last?
  The International Space Station was built.
  The first spacecraft traveled into space.
  The first person walked on the Moon.
- Which came second?
  The telephone was invented.
  The Internet was invented.
  The telegraph was invented.
- Which came last?
  Abraham Lincoln was U.S. president.
  John F. Kennedy was U.S. president.
  George Washington was U.S. president.
- Which came second?
  The first airplane flew.
  The Pilgrims landed at Plymouth Rock.
  World War II ended.
- Which came first?
  Cell phones were invented.
  Video games were invented.
  Electricity was discovered.

SOCIAL STUDIES   CULTURAL TRADITIONS

IT'S A TRADITION!

Remind students what a tradition is.

> A **tradition** is a behavior or set of behaviors followed repeatedly by a group of people from generation to generation.

Then use three minutes to name traditions. Ask students to quickly name one or more traditions connected to each of these events, situations, or times in a culture.

- raising children
- birthdays
- weddings
- national holidays
- dress or costumes
- family gatherings
- meals
- church services
- school
- celebrations
- sporting events
- religious holidays

Use another two or three minutes to brainstorm ideas for a class tradition. Ask students to think of a new tradition that they could begin in their classroom. Once a tradition is agreed upon, try to practice it daily, weekly, or at another regular interval throughout the rest of the school year.

5 Minute Warm-Ups for Elementary Grades, Rev. Ed.   ©2004 by Incentive Publications, Inc., Nashville, TN.

SOCIAL STUDIES   BARTER

NO MONEY

Review the definition of barter with your class.

> To **barter** is to exchange goods or services for other goods or services without the use of money.

Let students tell what goods or services they could exchange for any of the following goods or services provided by their parents:

- a trip to the beach
- a party for their friends
- a special outfit for a party
- a new compact disc
- transportation to a friend's house
- a new baseball glove
- a trip to Disneyland
- a pet
- help with homework
- a new video game

5 Minute Warm-Ups for Elementary Grades, Rev. Ed.   ©2004 by Incentive Publications, Inc., Nashville, TN.

SOCIAL STUDIES   ECONOMICS

IT ALL DEPENDS

Discuss the interdependence of jobs and products. Then name one of the following situations and have students name all the jobs and products that would be affected by the situation.

- No one wants to drink milk anymore.
- All of the world's tomato crops fail.
- All fresh water becomes contaminated with salt water.
- Rock music is banned from all public places.
- A uniform of black pants and white shirts is required to be worn by everyone at school and at work.
- Schools will be open only one or two days a week.

5 Minute Warm-Ups for Elementary Grades, Rev. Ed.   ©2004 by Incentive Publications, Inc., Nashville, TN.

SOCIAL STUDIES   CULTURAL SYMBOLS

FLAGS HAVE MEANING

Show students pictures of a few flags from states or countries. (The encyclopedia, world almanac, Internet, or social studies textbooks are good sources for nice, colorful pictures of flags.) Notice how different colors, symbols, pictures, or icons are used on flags. Point out the meaning of the colors and symbols on the U.S. flag.

Ask students to agree on 2–3 colors and 1–2 symbols that would fit the class. Discuss the meanings that the colors and symbols would have.

Later, when time permits, have students form small groups. Give each group a piece of paper large enough to be the size of a small flag, and ask them to design a class flag using the colors and symbols agreed upon. Let each group explain the meanings and design of the different flags. Enjoy seeing how different groups convey the same meaning.

5 Minute Warm-Ups for Elementary Grades, Rev. Ed.   ©2004 by Incentive Publications, Inc., Nashville, TN.

SOCIAL STUDIES   HISTORY

HISTORY IN THE NEWS

A good way to review historical events is to imagine how a newspaper would have reported the event when it happened. Ask students to think of important events they remember from the past. (This could be either the recent or distant past.) Encourage them to think about local and state events as well as national or world events.

Quickly discuss the way that newspaper headlines present an event (e.g., few words, incomplete sentences, catchy slogans). Let students work in pairs to write news headlines for the events they remember. Later, students might research to find the precise dates for their headlines.

Examples:
- Tornado Tears Up Town
- Women Can Vote, Finally
- Columbia Explodes in the Sky
- Big Steps on the Moon
- Third Graders Perform Smash Hit
- Daring Rescue Frees Prisoner of War

SOCIAL STUDIES   MANUFACTURING

TRACE IT

To help students realize that goods do not usually come straight from resources to consumers, let them trace one of the following products from raw materials to finished product. Keep them on track if they tend to skip steps in the process.

an ice cream bar	automobile
front door of house	shirt
jug of milk	computer
notebook paper	football
textbook	radio

SOCIAL STUDIES   MANUFACTURING

ON LINE

Many products are produced on assembly lines where each worker has one specialized job to do toward completion of the product.

Have students decide what workers would be needed to produce these products on an assembly line:

- homemade lemonade
- Halloween masks
- autograph books
- banana splits
- laminated placemats
- chocolate chip cookies
- peanut butter sandwiches
- terrariums with plants and insects

SOCIAL STUDIES   CARDINAL DIRECTIONS

SMALL STEPS—GIANT STEPS

Strengthen students' awareness of cardinal directions by taking actual steps in these directions. Label the four directions (N, S, E, W) with large letters on the appropriate walls of the classroom. (You might also add NE, NW, SE, and SW.) Make sure students look out the windows to gain a perspective of what lies in each direction from the classroom. Choose one student at a time. The student could begin in the center of the classroom, or anywhere else that you direct. Give an instruction such as one of these.

- Take 5 small steps east.
- Take 2 giant steps southwest.
- Take 7 small steps south. Whose desk do you reach?
- Take giant steps toward the northeast. How many steps will it take to reach a wall?
- Take 10 giant backward steps north.
- Whose desk is 3 giant steps to the west of you?
- Take 9 small steps backwards in a southeast direction.

LANGUAGE
LANGUAGE
LANGUAGE
LANGUAGE
LANGUAGE
LANGUAGE
LANGUAGE
LANGUAGE
LANGUAGE
LANGUAGE
LANGUAGE

CRAZY TALK

Idioms are an interesting part of our language. Read these to your students and let them discuss the meaning of each.

in the nick of time	on pins and needles
passed with flying colors	have butterflies in your stomach
hit it off great	in one ear and out the other
didn't see eye to eye	on your high horse
spring a leak	chip off the old block
bury the hatchet	kick the bucket
bring home the bacon	lost his head
go through the roof	back to square one

MONEY TALK

All the following sayings have to do with money. Let students discuss what they think each saying means. See if they can add other sayings to the list.

- "He is a penny pincher."
    (He doesn't want to spend money or is very careful/thrifty.)
- "It cost a pretty penny."
    (It was very expensive.)
- "It cost an arm and a leg."
    (It was very expensive.)
- "Money doesn't grow on trees."
    (Money has to be earned.)

LANGUAGE

PAST TENSES

SAY WHEN

It isn't easy to get children to use some past tense verbs correctly. They often don't "sound" right because we are used to hearing them used incorrectly. Occasionally, try a short drill with some of these often-misused verbs.

Present Today I . . .	Past Yesterday I . . .	Past Participle I have . . .
see	saw	seen
take	took	taken
draw	drew	drawn
teach	taught	taught
do	did	done
go	went	gone
eat	ate	eaten

LANGUAGE

TEXTBOOK INFORMATION

THE INSIDE STORY

Quickly review the parts of a textbook:

| title page | body of book | appendix |
| table of contents | glossary | index |

Ask students which part of the book they would use to:
- find the copyright date
- find the author and illustrator
- look up the meaning of a word in the text
- find what page a map is on
- find special charts, references, etc.

LANGUAGE   IMPROMPTU SPEAKING

THINK FAST!

Impromptu speaking gives students a chance to think on their feet. Select one of the subjects below. Call on one student to talk on this subject for about one minute. Select a different subject for the next student. Add other subjects to the list for future talks.

Suggested subjects:

- You are a clock on the classroom wall. Describe your day.
- You are the principal of your school for today. What will you do?
- You are a pilgrim on the Mayflower. Tell about your trip.
- You will make all decisions about your family's meals for one week. Tell us about your decisions.

LANGUAGE   SYNONYMS

10-SECOND SYNONYMS

Stimulate students to do some quick thinking while they sharpen their vocabulary skills. Tell them that you will call out a word. They will have ten seconds to think of a word with a similar meaning (a synonym). If they can think of more than one word in 10 seconds—that's great!

- great
- entire
- steal
- simple

- ruin
- grab
- prevent
- wild

- munch
- weary
- scratchy
- frightening

- burglar
- huge
- yelled
- mighty

54

LANGUAGE   SENTENCES

STRETCH-A-SENTENCE

Make ordinary sentences more interesting and informative by stretching them! Practice sentence skills at the same time. Write a short sentence on the board, or read it to students. Give them one minute to expand the sentence so that it is more interesting, more colorful, or more informative. Encourage them to change the sentence form (rearrange words, turn a sentence into a question, or add phrases).

Examples:
- Sam got ready and left for school.
- After eating a scrumptious breakfast, Sam tossed his books and supplies into his backpack and headed out the door—all ready to race after the school bus.

Other sentences to expand:
- Did you hear that noise?
- We watched tigers at the zoo.
- Tom ordered lunch.
- That music is so loud!

LANGUAGE   WORD FORMATION

GRAND SLAM!

Write one of these word family bases on the board. Ask for a student volunteer to "come to bat" with this word base.

Let the student score a single hit if he or she can add a blend to the base, a double hit if a suffix is then added, a triple hit if a prefix is also added, and a grand slam if the student can spell the final word. Then bring another student "up to bat."

Word Family Bases:

ump	ail	ope	ake	ape	on
eep	ick	oat	ent	ack	id

 LANGUAGE  SYLLABLES

SYLLABLE RELAY

Separate the class into two teams. Ask for a one-syllable word from the first team. Then ask for a two-syllable word from the second team. Continue to alternate back and forth between the two teams, increasing the number of syllables each time.

Whenever a team cannot answer on its turn, the other team scores a point. Whichever team began second in the first round will begin first in the second round. Play for a pre-determined length of time or until one team scores a set number of points.

Don't be surprised to find kids going through the dictionary in their spare time. They will want to be ready if they know they can play again soon.

 LANGUAGE  TOPIC SELECTION

TOPIC TREASURES

Many times children find it difficult to begin writing a story or report because their topics are too broad.

Give students one of these broad topics and ask them to help you think of all possible related narrow topics.

Topics:

all about fish	TV shows	famous women	races
trains	inventions	music	careers
team sports	horses	automobiles	the space age

LANGUAGE   HOMONYMS

WORDS THAT CONFUSE

Prepare two signs before class, each having a misused homonym. Then use the signs for an activity that will help clear up confusion between words that sound alike.

| Yummy tacos sold hear | SANDWICHES 75 sense each |

Show students the signs. Discuss how the words were used incorrectly and replace wrong words with correct ones. Then, divide students into small groups, giving a piece of poster board or drawing paper to each group. Ask them to make a sign that uses a wrong homonym in place of the correct one. When time permits, let groups share their signs with the class and discuss corrections.

- Beware of dog waying 180 pounds
- Ski goggles on sale for only ate dollars
- Sign up write now for free guitar lessons
- Come sea the dancing tigers
- Wood anyone like a free puppy?
- Fresh corn groan here

LANGUAGE   DESCRIPTIVE LANGUAGE

LOOKING GOOD

Have students practice using good descriptive words with this activity. Select one distinctive character or person from the following list. Whisper that name to one student. That student must try to describe the character or person to the rest of the class without telling what the person or character does, or the specific name.

Superman	any popular musician
Santa Claus	Cupid
Abraham Lincoln	Statue of Liberty
George Washington	any popular television character
any popular cartoon character	

LANGUAGE   COMMUNICATION

GOSSIP CHAIN

Use the old gossip chain game to show your students how things get changed as they are repeated over and over. Innocent people get hurt or may be embarrassed when facts are distorted.

Start one of these rumors to be whispered student to student around the room. Most will end up changed enough to make the point: spreading gossip is harmful.

- Susie isn't friends with Janey anymore because Janey cheated off of Susie's test (will probably end up that Susie cheated off of Janey).
- Johnny got suspended from school because he was in a fight that started in Mr. White's room (will probably end up that Johnny started the fight).

LANGUAGE   CONTEXT

BIG WORDS MADE EASY

Take the mystery out of big words by putting them into context. Say a big word. Then read it in a sentence. Ask students to listen carefully to figure out what the word means from the way it is used in the sentence.

Examples:

- interrogation: During the hour-long interrogation, the detective asked Lacey over 50 questions about what she saw and did the night of the robbery.
- meticulously: Tad did his work so meticulously that everything was finished perfectly in order, on time, and with no mistakes.
- octogenarian: Grandpa George, age 85, had lunch with his other octogenarian friends: Charlie, age 81, Lucy, age 89, Hank, age 87, and Frank, age 83.

 LANGUAGE  WRITING

ALL ABOUT ME

Ask each student to write a brief description of him- or herself on a piece of paper. Have them pass the papers to you. Read aloud the description and see if the rest of the class can identify the student. Be sure to include a description of yourself.

This activity can be extended by assigning a number to each paper. Post the descriptions on a bulletin board. Let each student number a paper to match the numbers on the descriptions. Then, through the day or over several days, students can list the students' names next to the number they think matches his or her description. Identify the correct names and let each student see how many he or she guessed correctly.

 LANGUAGE  ANALOGIES

FINISH THIS!

Solving an analogy is a process that makes use of many skills: vocabulary, grammar, word use, spelling, and reasoning. See how many of these analogies students can finish in 5 minutes. You can read them aloud, and have students finish them orally. Be aware that there may be more than one correct way to finish some of them. If time permits, talk about the pattern of the different analogies.
(Read them: "Mouse is to mice as child is to what?")

mouse : mice as child: ____
hurry : hurried as fly: ____
fingers : typing as feet: ____
ten : twenty as five: ____
champ : tramp as chuck: ____
cold : freezing as warm: ____
beater : mixing as spatula: ____

lungs : breathing as stomach: ____
TV : news as CD player: ____
infant : child as teenager: ____
extraordinary : ordinary as superhuman: ____
work : vacation as hungry: ____
nervous : relaxed as grumpy: ____
lawyer : courtroom as doctor: ____

LANGUAGE  POETRY

POEMS IN A MINUTE

Formula poetry is easy to write and great for a class project. As you read aloud the requirement for a line, let the students decide what to write. Write it on the board as they compose it together.

Example:
  Line 1: What are you writing about? Butterflies.
  Line 2: Two adjectives to describe it. Colorful and bright.
  Line 3: Two adverbs to tell how it acts. Quietly, softly.
  Line 4: Two verbs to tell about it. Flying and fluttering.
  Line 5: Tell how it makes you feel. Makes me feel free.
  Line 6: Repeat what you're writing about. Butterflies.

LANGUAGE  WORD CHOICE

OTHER WAYS TO SAY IT

Some words are used too much, particularly in written work. Encourage young writers to avoid ordinary or over-used words by substituting more specific or colorful words in their place. For each over-used word below, give students about 20 seconds to brainstorm 5 or more other words that could be used instead— words that are more unique or interesting.

- wonderful
- walked
- moving
- cold
- scared

- pretty
- tasty
- ate
- good
- big

- red
- tired
- happy
- interesting
- yelled

LANGUAGE   RELATED WORDS

WEBBING WORDS

Write one word on the board. Ask students to think of synonyms, antonyms, or just words that are related to that word. As they name the type of words specified, add them to the board as a web around the original word.

Example: Healthy (name synonyms)

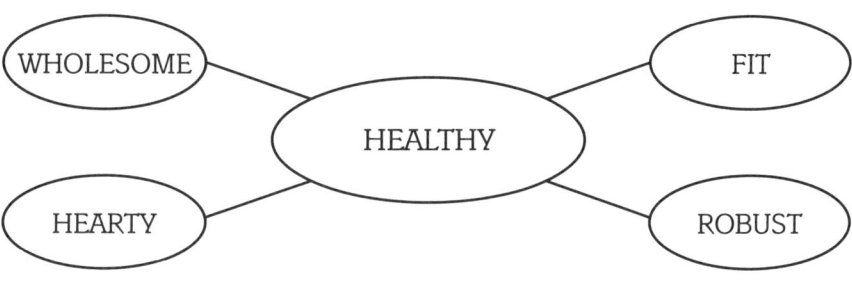

LANGUAGE   WORD INTERPRETATION

MOODY WORDS

Let students take turns showing how they would look and act if one of these moody words described them.

frustrated	excited	embarrassed
cheerful	scared	defeated
angry	bewildered	proud
sad	ashamed	happy

LANGUAGE  WORD USAGE

FILL IT FAST!

Quickly sketch a five-by-five square grid on the board. Make each section large enough to be able to write one word inside.

Ask students for a five-letter word to write above the squares of the grid horizontally. Then select a category to write next to each square vertically down the left side.

Challenge students to think of words to fit the categories that start with each of the letters of the horizontal word. Fill in the grid with the students' words as quickly as possible. Keep track of their record time and try to beat it the next time you play.

Categories: food, clothing, boys' or girls' names, states, rivers, animals, automobiles, TV shows, countries, or games

 LANGUAGE  LISTENING

WHAT ABOUT ERNIE?

Sharpen listening skills with a short exercise that focuses on listening to this poem about Ernie. Read the poem. Then ask students questions such as these:

- What did the sign say?
- With what was the sand filled?
- What was the quicksand like?
- How many people went to find Ernie?
- How did Ernie get out?
- What words described the quicksand?

> Ernie stepped in quicksand
> Even though the sign was there.
> He walked into the middle
> Though the sign told him, "Beware!"
>
> The sand was filled with water,
> Which turned it into muck
> All wet and thick and gooey.
> Poor Ernie was out of luck.
>
> His feet sank in up to his knees.
> He tried to run on through.
> He grabbed and pulled and hollered,
> But the quicksand was like glue.
>
> We all went out to find him.
> We heard a muffled shout.
> We threw a rope, and just in time
> We pulled poor Ernie out.

LANGUAGE   REFERENCE SKILLS

SEEK AND FIND

To know everything is not possible, but to know where to find information about everything is important. This activity provides practice in selecting appropriate reference works for specific tasks.

Ask students to tell what reference work would be the best place to find the following information:

- population of your state
- name of the team that won the world series last year
- the author of <u>Charlotte's Web</u>
- a picture of a persimmon
- the year that Thomas Edison was born
- who invented the typewriter
- the highest mountain in the United States
- how to pronounce "rendezvous"

LANGUAGE   WORD FORMATION

ALPHABET SOUP

1. Call on eight to ten students and ask each to give you a letter of the alphabet. Write the letters on the board as they are announced.

2. Give the class two minutes to make as many words as possible with the letters listed. Write them on the board as they call them out.

   Variation: Keep a set of index cards with one letter per card. Shuffle the deck and randomly select eight letters to write on the board. Proceed with Step 2 above.

LANGUAGE   FACTS AND OPINIONS

PROVE IT

Is it a fact or an opinion? Students often think that familiar opinions are actually fact. In this activity, students must decide whether each statement is an opinion or a fact. If they think it is a fact, they must be able to tell how to prove it. Try these:

- Canada and the United States share a border.
- Ice cream melts.
- Most students prefer chocolate milk to white milk.
- Roses smell good.
- _____ is a great singer. (Fill in name of any popular singer.)
- Solar energy can be used to cook hot dogs.

Add others to the list or let students add other statements.

LANGUAGE   WRITING

SHARP SENSES

Good writing uses words that appeal to many senses. Think about a topic with the class. Work to write 5 different sentences about the topic—one sentence that appeals to each of the different senses. You might work with topics such as a baseball game, a dark night, a birthday party, a school lunchroom, fireworks, or a blizzard.

Example: Topic—The Circus
- Sight: Silly clowns with floppy green shoes and raggedy suits turned somersaults.
- Smell: The scent of buttery popcorn floats on the air all the way to my nose.
- Touch: Watching the tightrope walker slip on the rope caused goose bumps to stand up all over my arms and legs!
- Hearing: The sharp crack of the lion tamer's whip seems to split the air.
- Taste: That tangy lemonade is so tart that it pinches my tongue.

LANGUAGE  SELF-EXPRESSION

IF I HAD . . .

Ask students to complete one of these "If I had" statements:

If I had . . .

    curly hair . . .

    two different-sized feet . . .

    $10,000 . . .

    11 brothers and sisters . . .

    nothing to do tomorrow . . .

    only one wish . . .

    a day to spend anywhere I wanted to . . .

LANGUAGE   COINING WORDS

DOUBLE TROUBLE

There are lots of double words that sound funny. Can your students think of all these and more?

Nana	dodo
mama	murmur
tutu	muumuu
tartar	yoyo

Let students make up double words and give their own meanings for them.

Example:

Yukyuk means a spinach dish for lunch.

LANGUAGE   WORD PLAY

DESCRIPTION DILEMMA

Have students name an interesting animal or object, or select one from the list below. Write the name of the object on the board vertically. Students should think of verbs to describe how it might move (if it's an animal) or adjectives to describe the object itself. Think of one for each letter in the name of the object.

Example: H-A-M-S-T-E-R

<u>h</u>armless   <u>m</u>ild-mannered   <u>t</u>errific   <u>r</u>estless
<u>a</u>ctive   <u>s</u>illy   <u>e</u>nergetic

Other word choices:

dinosaur   unicorn   computer
leprechaun   dragon   ostrich
bullfrog   platypus   ghost

LANGUAGE   COMMUNICATION

BOYS AND GIRLS

Lead a discussion of the advantages and disadvantages of being a boy or being a girl. Have girls tell what they consider the advantages of being a girl. Let them tell the disadvantages or problems with being female.

Then let boys discuss any advantages or disadvantages of being a boy.

Be sure to give both the boys and girls equal time to state their opinions.

LANGUAGE   ALLITERATION

COUNTING FUN

Put some fun into oral counting practice. Count from one to the number of students in class. Pair each number with a phrase using alliteration. Use a descriptive word and a noun with each number.

Example:

> One Wonderful Waffle
>
> Two Terrible Tempers
>
> Three Thirsty Thumbs
>
> Four Ferocious Footballs

LANGUAGE   WORD FORMATION

ALL IN THE FAMILY

List one of these word family bases on the board. Have students call out as many words as they can that use this word base. Remind them to use blends, prefixes, suffixes, and plural endings to make new words.

-at	-ick
-it	-ack
-all	-act
-ill	-ad
-ot	-ate

LANGUAGE TABLE OF CONTENTS

SCAVENGER HUNT

Help students become familiar with their textbooks and practice using a table of contents. Have students take out a specific textbook and open it to the table of contents.

Ask questions like the ones listed here:
- What is the title of chapter three?
- On what page does Chapter Four begin?
- How many chapters are in this book?
- What chapter has information about _____ (topic in that book)?
- Is there an appendix?
- Is there a glossary? If so, on what page does it start?

LANGUAGE ASSOCIATED WORDS

WORD PAIRS

Some words just always seem to be found together in our language. See how many of these word pairs students are familiar with. Give the first part of the pair and let students supply the rest.

- cup and <u>saucer</u>
- bright-eyed and <u>bushy-tailed</u>
- sugar and <u>spice</u>
- strange but <u>true</u>
- spic and <u>span</u>
- huff and <u>puff</u>
- hide and <u>seek</u>
- peace and <u>quiet</u>
- sticks and <u>stones</u>
- aches and <u>pains</u>

If these are too easy, try a few word triplets:
- bacon, <u>lettuce</u>, and <u>tomato</u>
- hop, <u>skip</u>, and <u>jump</u>
- animal, <u>vegetable</u>, or <u>mineral</u>
- tall, <u>dark</u>, and <u>handsome</u>

LANGUAGE   CATEGORIZING

YELLOW IS FOR JELLO?

To practice categorizing objects, select a color or shape and ask students to name as many things as they can that would normally be that color or shape. Keep going until no one can think of another object in that category. Some students will really stretch their imaginations (and yours).

Possible Categories:

- things that are green . . . grass, money, spinach, mold
- things that are round . . . sun, oranges, clock, zero
- things that are red . . . strawberries, blood, roses, tired eyes
- things that are rectangular . . . tissue box, textbook, door, window

LANGUAGE   DICTIONARY SKILLS

IN THE MIDDLE

Write one of these pairs of guide words on the board. Ask students to name all the words they can think of that would fit on a dictionary page between those guide words. If anyone challenges a word offered, write that word on the board between the guide words so the class can decide if it belongs there.

Guide word pairs:

sand .... slide	help .... house	laugh .... lint
baby .... bed	you .... zip	stutter .... swift
pin .... plant	bullet .... cent	act .... art
tea .... train	man .... middle	fast .... fence

LANGUAGE   GENERAL KNOWLEDGE

HEAD OF THE LINE

Have students line up somewhere in the room. Starting with the last student in the line, ask for an example from one of the language categories given below. If the student is able to give an example that is correct, that student moves to the head of the line. Change categories frequently within the five-minute period.

  a contraction   a noun
  a prefix   an abbreviation
  a suffix   a word beginning with QU
  a preposition   a compound word
  an adverb   a pair of homonyms
  a word with Z   a word and its antonym

LANGUAGE   CREATIVE THINKING

UNCOMMONLY GOOD

Select a common item that is well-known by almost all the students. Discuss its common uses. Then encourage students to use their imaginations in thinking of uncommon ways to use the item.

Examples: **toothbrush (Common use: for brushing teeth)**

  Uncommon uses: to brush a hamster, to scrub potatoes, to clean jewelry, as a hockey stick for a squirrel

Other commonalities to try:

  safety pin   toothpick   pencil   paper clip
  fork   spoon   tissue   tack
  nail file   comb   broom   straw

LANGUAGE   SELF-EXPRESSION

WONDER-FULL

Encourage students to vocalize their "I wonder . . ." thoughts. Let each student tell one thing about which he or she wonders. The thoughts may be serious or they may be on the silly side.

If time permits, write these thoughts on a large sheet of poster board or craft paper for the bulletin board. Students can continue to add to the list. They can also write great creative stories based on the wonder list.

I wonder . . .

> . . . how many stars there are
> . . . why the colors in the rainbow are always in the same order
> . . . why my parents picked this name for me
> . . . which really came first—the chicken or the egg?
> . . . what my teacher does after school

LANGUAGE   CAUSE AND EFFECT

WHAT HAPPENED?

Have students examine cause and effect relationships by completing these statements to tell what happened next.

> I was so hungry that. . .
> Strong winds blew and . . .
> I felt sick so I . . .
> Jack put hot fudge sauce on the ice cream and it . . .

Now change the activity around. Have students finish the same statements so that the part they add is the cause rather than the effect:

> I was hungry because . . .
> Strong winds blew when . . .
> I felt sick after . . .
> Jack put hot fudge sauce on the ice cream because . . .

LANGUAGE   WORD USAGE

SEASONAL SEARCH

When it is time to line up, let each student earn a place in line by giving you a vocabulary word that is appropriate for the current season or holiday. Example:

    Fall: leaves, autumn, pumpkin, witch, Halloween

    Winter: Christmas, snow, cold, icicles, sled

Lists could also be made for a particular subject or unit that you are currently studying.

To extend the activity, as each student gives a word, ask for a volunteer to spell the word.

LANGUAGE   IRREGULAR PLURALS

MOUSE, MICE . . . HOUSE, HICE?

Irregular words are something hard for students to remember. Use this list to review irregular plurals. Call out the singular form of the word and ask students to name the plural form.

mouse . . . mice	die . . . dice
goose . . . geese	child . . . children
fish . . . fish or fishes	woman . . . women
deer . . . deer	cactus . . . cacti

SCIENCE
SCIENCE
SCIENCE
SCIENCE
SCIENCE
SCIENCE
SCIENCE
SCIENCE
SCIENCE
SCIENCE
SCIENCE

SCIENCE FIELDS OF SCIENCE

SO MANY SCIENCES!

Get students to think about the many different things and subjects studied by scientists. See how many of these fields of science are familiar to students. Ask them to describe what a scientist in each of these fields might study. (If students do not know about a particular field, use the activity as an opportunity to give them some new information.)

- botany (plants)
- ecology (environment)
- biology (living things)
- geology (Earth)
- zoology (animals)
- ornithology (birds)
- ichthyology (fish)
- meteorology (weather)
- genetics (inherited traits)
- chemistry (combinations of matter)
- physics (matter, force, energy)
- oceanography (the ocean)
- anatomy (structure of living things)
- astronomy (stars & outer space)
- microbiology (tiny living things)
- marine biology (living things in the ocean)

5 Minute Warm-Ups for Elementary Grades, Rev. Ed. ©2004 by Incentive Publications, Inc., Nashville, TN.

SCIENCE HISTORY OF SCIENCE

WHAT A DIFFERENCE!

Scientific discoveries and inventions have made great differences in life on Earth. Ask students to think about how these things have changed things in the world. See how many differences they can name for these discoveries or inventions.

- discovery of cells
- invention of email
- discovery of salt
- invention of mathematics
- discovery of radio waves
- invention of refrigerators
- invention of fire
- invention of jet engines
- invention of the camera
- discovery of X-rays
- discovery that the Earth is round
- building of pyramids

If time permits, students can think of other amazing discoveries or inventions, and describe the difference each one has made.

5 Minute Warm-Ups for Elementary Grades, Rev. Ed. ©2004 by Incentive Publications, Inc., Nashville, TN.

SCIENCE   HISTORY OF SCIENCE

GREAT DISCOVERIES

See how many of these discoveries students can name. Tell the class that you will describe a discovery or invention. It's their job to name it! What's the discovery (or invention)?

- a way to show Earth's surface on paper .... (maps)
- a special tube for seeing extremely tiny objects .... (microscope)
- something that helps people recover from infections .... (antibiotics or medicine)
- something that helps people keep food from spoiling ..... (refrigerator or freezer)
- a round object that changed transportation forever .... (wheel)
- a special tube to see things long distances away .... (telescope)
- a force that pulls things to the ground .... (gravity)
- something to write on other than stone or wood .... (paper)
- a device that carries a human voice across a wire .... (telephone)
- something that allows doctors to listen to a heartbeat .... (stethoscope)

5 Minute Warm-Ups for Elementary Grades, Rev. Ed.   ©2004 by Incentive Publications, Inc., Nashville, TN.

SCIENCE   SCIENCE APPLICATIONS

SCIENCE IN EVERY ROOM

Science can be found all around the house! Students often think that science is something done in school. It is fun (and important) for them to realize how much science is a part of everyday life. Write the name of one of the following rooms or places on each of seven large pieces of paper (such as mural or drawing paper).

Divide students into seven groups. Give one piece of paper to each group. Ask students to draw things that show ways that science can be found in that room. They will have to work quickly to show as many examples of science as they can in the short time. Allow time later for each group to share and explain results.

- kitchen
- living room
- swimming pool
- bathroom
- garage
- bedroom
- office
- playroom (or basement)
- attic

5 Minute Warm-Ups for Elementary Grades, Rev. Ed.   ©2004 by Incentive Publications, Inc., Nashville, TN.

SCIENCE CAUSE AND EFFECT

LOOKING FOR CAUSES

The cause-effect relationship shows up often in science. It is a major concept for students to notice and examine.

Read each example of a cause to students. Ask them to think about what the effect might be. (There may be more than one effect for each cause.)

- Cause: Mac leaves his bicycle out in the rain for 2 weeks. Effect: _____
- Cause: Lana falls from her skateboard and scrapes her knees badly. Effect: _____
- Cause: A predator comes close to a nest of baby birds. Effect: _____
- Cause: A storm sends huge waves dashing against the shore. Effect: _____
- Cause: Tracy throws a handful of popcorn kernels into a fire. Effect: _____
- Cause: Water from the sprinkler only reaches the center of the lawn. Effect: _____

5 Minute Warm-Ups for Elementary Grades, Rev. Ed.   ©2004 by Incentive Publications, Inc., Nashville, TN.

SCIENCE FORM AND FUNCTION

WHAT GOOD ARE WHISKERS?

The form (shape, size, color, or appearance) of an object is often a key to what the object can do or how it can be used (its function). This form-function relationship is a key concept in science. Discuss this idea with students by asking them to think about the form and function of these objects.

object	form	function
• cat's whiskers	long, sensitive	help cat feel things around it
• elbow	hinged joint	allows it to bend
• flower petals	_____	_____
• dandelion fluff	_____	_____
• lobster claw	_____	_____
• bike helmet	_____	_____
• cactus	_____	_____
• duck's feet	_____	_____

5 Minute Warm-Ups for Elementary Grades, Rev. Ed.   ©2004 by Incentive Publications, Inc., Nashville, TN.

 SCIENCE  CLASSIFICATION

CLASSY SCIENCE

Brush up on classification skills and listening skills at the same time. Tell students to listen carefully as each list of objects is read. They should try to figure out why these items are classified into the same group. Then, without saying the name of the group, they should try to add one or two other items to each group.

- starfish, eel, coral, seaweed, dolphin (things that live in the sea)
- lungs, ribs, small intestine, ear lobes, liver (parts of the human body)
- river, ocean, lake, stream, pond (bodies of water)
- centimeter, inch, meter, mile, foot (units for measuring length or distance)
- crocodile, lizard, rattlesnake, alligator (reptiles)
- fog, blizzard, tornado, hurricane, thunderstorm (weather conditions)
- sequoia, dandelion, pine, cedar, maple, oak (kinds of trees)

 SCIENCE  OBSERVATION

PAY ATTENTION!

To observe means to pay attention to facts and occurrences. To be good observers, students need to use all their senses as they try to learn about things. Give students a series of instructions for simple activities. Tell them to use all their senses. Ask them to name the senses that helped them in each observation. Things to have ready for the observations: 3 peeled hard-boiled eggs and a fork, a slice of green banana for each student, and one can of soda pop

- Press 2 fingers lightly against the side of your neck next to your Adam's apple. What do you observe?
- Rub your hands together hard and fast. What do you observe?
- What do you observe as I smash these hard-boiled eggs? (Gather students closely around as you do this.)
- What do you observe as you taste this slice of green banana?
- I'm shaking a can of soda pop. Now I'm opening it. What do you observe?

SCIENCE   LIFE CHARACTERISTICS

IS IT ALIVE?

"How can you tell if something is alive?" Ask students this question. Listen to their ideas, discuss them, and make a list. Then test some objects against their list (for example: a bug, rock, leaf, dried flowers, cookie, air, apple, fossil, etc.) As they name objects or items, ask of each one: "According to your list, is this alive?" Keep discussing and altering the list until students have arrived at an understanding of all the life characteristics.

Examples:
- uses food and water
- takes in air
- grows
- gives off waste
- responds to things in the environment
- makes more organisms like itself (reproduces)

SCIENCE   LIFE CLASSIFICATION

IN THE WRONG PLACE

Remind students that living things are classified into groups. Each group shares some common characteristics. Read each of the following lists. Tell students to listen carefully for the organism that does NOT fit with all the others in the group. After they identify the "imposter," they might attempt to name or describe the class into which all the others fit.

- crocodile, turtle, hummingbird*, python, lizard, alligator (reptiles)
- mushroom*, petunia, pansy, lilac, daisy, rose, tulip (flowering plants)
- shark, minnow, octopus*, whale, trout, salmon (fish)
- blue jay, penguin, ostrich, raven, starfish*, robin (birds)
- frog, iguana*, tadpole, toad, salamander (amphibians)
- snail*, tiger, monkey, rabbit, mouse, zebra (mammals)

 **SCIENCE**  ANIMAL MOVEMENT

ON THE MOVE

What animal can hop, skip, leap, crawl, and climb? See if students can name one animal that can do all these things. (A human can!) One of the characteristics that makes animals different from plants is that animals **move**. Animals move in many different ways. Ask students to name as many animals as they can that move in each of the following ways. Allow about 15 seconds to collect animal names for each movement.

- slither
- crawl
- climb
- fly
- pounce

- walk
- slink
- hop
- swim
- dive

- run
- gallop
- swoop
- leap
- slide

 **SCIENCE**  HABITATS

HOME SWEET HOME

Plants and animals have homes, too. Each one has a place that is comfortable for it to live. The home of any living organism provides things it needs to live, grow, reproduce, and be healthy. Write the names of some homes on the board. Give each student a large piece of drawing paper. Ask them to choose a home from the list and quickly draw some plants and animals that would live in that home. Later, you might combine ideas to make larger murals of different biomes.

- grassland
- tree trunk
- puddle
- tide pool
- coral reef

- rainforest
- your backyard
- pine forest
- desert
- Arctic area

SCIENCE  OCEANS

WE KNOW THIS!

Students probably know more about the ocean than they realize. Ask them to start thinking of what they know. Remind them to think about all aspects of the ocean: plant life, animal life, the water, water movements, the shoreline, the ocean bottom. Then, take turns making statements about what they know. Begin every statement with, "I know this."

Examples:
- I know this: Ocean waves break near the shore.
- I know this: It is very dark in the deepest part of the ocean.
- I know this: Oysters live in the ocean.
- I know this: There are whole mountains under the ocean.
- I know this: Seaweed has hollow tubes that help it float on the ocean surface.
- I know this: Tiny animals build coral reefs on the ocean floor.

SCIENCE EARTH SCIENCE

GEO-TALK

Write "Earth words" such as those listed below on separate slips of paper. Give one slip to a pair of students. Ask them to think about how they would describe this event or object without using its name. Tell them that they may not use any part of the word in giving clues. Give them a few minutes to come up with a plan. Then, use small spaces of time over the next day or so for each pair to give clues to the class about their word, while the rest of the class tries to guess the Earth-related object or event.

- gravity
- earthquake
- erupt
- rocks
- volcano
- sand dune
- aftershock
- fault
- lava
- mud slide
- erosion
- glacier
- river bed
- flood
- geyser

SCIENCE   SOLAR SYSTEM

JOIN THE SOLAR SYSTEM

One of the best ways for students to gain an understanding of the solar system is to "become" the solar system. Make labels (shown below) of bodies in the solar system.

Pin one of the labels on each student. Give them several minutes to arrange themselves correctly into a "human solar system!" If possible, give the "Sun" a lantern or other light source and make the room dark. Let students try out the movements of the solar system (rotation of planets, revolution of planets and Moon).

Labels:
- Sun
- Mercury
- Venus
- Earth
- Mars
- Jupiter
- Saturn
- Uranus
- Neptune
- Pluto
- Moon
- comet
- asteroids (make several)
- stars (make several)

SCIENCE   SPACE SCIENCE

WORDS FROM OUTER SPACE

Get warmed up for studying space science by building a collection of outer space words. Ask students to brainstorm all the words they have heard that have to do with space. Encourage them to think of naming words (nouns), describing words (adjectives) and action words (verbs). Later, use this word collection as the basis for a space science lesson or writing experience.

Examples:
- launch
- streak
- planet
- Moon
- Sun
- black
- satellite
- explosion
- sparkle
- star
- brilliance
- solar flare
- revolve
- rocket
- black hole
- meteor
- meteorites
- shooting star
- radiant
- wormhole
- supernova
- comet
- astronaut
- asteroid

SCIENCE   SENSES

SENSATIONAL SCIENCE

Use this chart to do a quick "sense activity." Draw this on the board ahead of time. Ask students to come and put an X in the box for each sense that is used during the activity listed. If time permits, have students add other activities to the chart.

Activity	Sight	Hearing	Smell	Touch	Taste
1. Eating ice cream					
2. Playing a drum					
3. Scraping your knee					
4. Taking a bath					
5. Listening to music					
6. Hugging a teddy bear					
7.					
8.					

5 Minute Warm-Ups for Elementary Grades, Rev. Ed.   ©2004 by Incentive Publications, Inc., Nashville, TN

SCIENCE   BODY PARTS AND PROCESSES

BODY JOBS

Each part or system of the human body has a very important job to do. When any part does not do its job well, the body can have trouble! Read the following "body jobs" aloud. Tell students to name the part or system that does each job. (Answers may vary. More than one part may be involved in a job!)

- breathe oxygen to body cells (lungs)
- dissolves food in the mouth (saliva)
- keeps dust out of eyes (eyelids)
- directs all body activities (brain)
- lets light into the eye (pupil)
- pumps blood through body (heart)
- lets the body feel hot or cold (skin)

5 Minute Warm-Ups for Elementary Grades, Rev. Ed.   ©2004 by Incentive Publications, Inc., Nashville, TN

SCIENCE DISEASES AND DISORDERS

BODY ALERT

Tell the class that you know someone named Charlie who has a lot of body ailments. Share Charlie's complaints with the class, one ailment at a time. Ask the class to name the disease or problem that Charlie might be describing. If time permits, let students identify and describe 10 more diseases or disorders.

- The amount of blood flowing to Charlie's brain was reduced and he fell over. (fainting)
- Charlie has an infection in his lungs. (bronchitis or pneumonia)
- Charlie's eyes and nose are itching and twitching. (allergy)
- There is a hole in Charlie's tooth caused by tooth decay. (cavity)
- A dog bit Charlie! He might have contracted a terrible virus disease! (rabies)
- Charlie hopped off his scooter and twisted his ankle joint way too far! (sprain)
- Charlie's body temperature is 5 degrees above normal. (fever)

SCIENCE HUMAN BODY

BONE SMART

Give each student a sheet with 10 small, blank stickers. Write the names of the following bones on the board, and ask students to copy the names onto their stickers, one per sticker. Or, have the names of the bones written on the stickers ahead of time. Then, direct the students to stick the stickers on their own bodies in the location of each bone. This is a good opportunity to teach the real names of the bones and the locations of any that are not known to students. Use either the simple or correct names of the bones.

- skull (head bone)
- patella (knee bone)
- fibula (shin bone)
- pelvis (hip bone)
- ribs
- scapula (shoulder blade)
- clavicle (collar bone)
- sternum (breast bone)
- spine (backbone)
- phalanges (finger bones)
- femur (thigh bone)
- humerus (upper arm)

SCIENCE PROPERTIES OF MATTER

MATTER MATTERS

Every kind of matter has properties or characteristics. Introduce this list of properties which belong to different substances. See if students can give at least two examples of objects or substances for each property—you might challenge them to give as many as 5 examples for each!

Properties:
- is solid
- is a liquid
- is a gas
- is magnetic
- flows
- is a mixture
- can float
- is a living substance
- is made up of more than one substance
- has weight greater than yours
- has less weight than a tennis ball
- used to be a living substance

SCIENCE CHANGES IN MATTER

MATTER CHANGES

Explain to students the two different kinds of changes that can take place in matter: physical and chemical. Ask students to discuss each of these changes, trying to decide if the change is a physical or chemical change. In a physical change, matter may change form or appearance, but it is still the same substance. In a chemical change, a substance actually changes into a different substance.

- You mix powder with milk to make chocolate milk. (P)
- Cake mix turns into cake when baked. (C)
- An egg becomes hard when boiled. (P)
- Bread molds after a few weeks. (C)
- A wet towel dries on the clothesline. (P)
- A mirror breaks. (P)
- You whip cream with a mixer. (P)
- Salt dissolves in water. (P)
- A snowman melts. (P)
- Your body digests food. (C)
- You fry an egg. (C)
- You bleach your hair. (C)
- A candle burns. (C)
- Meat freezes in the freezer. (P)
- Your bicycle rusts outdoors. (P)

SCIENCE   WATER AND FLOATING

WILL IT FLOAT?

Have a dishpan full of water ready for this quick game. Ask students to look around the room and choose small objects. For each one, ask, "Will it float?" Let students hypothesize about the answer to the question for each objects. Then, test each item. Have students keep a list or chart with the "guesses" and the final outcomes of each test.

Examples of objects to test:
- sponge
- ruler
- wadded-up paper
- eraser
- index card
- plastic spoon
- stick of gum
- flat piece of paper
- paper clip
- pencil
- tack
- shoestring
- ring
- staple
- hair clip

SCIENCE   FIELDS OF SCIENCE

KNOW YOUR "-OLOGIES!"

How many fields of science can your students identify correctly? Call out the name of a scientific field, then give students a few seconds to tell what is studied within that field.

- anthropology (cultures)
- archaeology (past cultures)
- bacteriology (bacteria)
- biology (living things)
- cardiology (heart function)
- climatology (climate)
- entomology (insects)
- geology (Earth's surface)
- ichthyology (fish)
- meteorology (weather)
- microbiology (microorganisms)
- mineralogy (minerals)
- ornithology (birds)
- paleontology (prehistoric life)
- seismology (earthquakes)
- zoology (animals)

SCIENCE   WEATHER CONDITIONS

WEATHER-WATCHING

Pretend that you are a weather forecaster predicting tomorrow's weather. Ask students to listen carefully to your forecasts, because you will not use the specific words to name the weather conditions. They will have to do that after hearing your description! If time permits, let a student be the weather person and describe a weather condition for others to name.

Sample "forecasts:"
- Electricity will be released from the clouds, rain will be heavy, and loud noises will come from the clouds. (thunderstorm)
- Little water droplets in clouds will hang close to the ground, making it hard to see. (fog)
- Water will freeze in layers around small balls of ice that will blow up and down during a terrible thunderstorm. (hailstorm)
- There will be heavy snow blown by high winds. (blizzard)
- Storms with very high winds will form over warm ocean water. (hurricane)

SCIENCE   MEASUREMENT

WHICH UNIT?

Do your students really understand the difference between the various units of measurement? Give them practice in using measurement concepts by asking them these questions.

"What unit of measurement would you use to measure . . ."

- the length of your nose?
- the weight of a full trash can?
- the height of your house?
- the weight of a mosquito?
- the width of a sidewalk?
- the temperature of coffee?
- the weight of an elephant?
- the amount of water in a bathtub?
- the distance from New York to Chicago?
- the amount of milkshake in your glass?

SCIENCE  ELECTRICITY

HURRAY FOR ELECTRICITY!

This quick and simple activity will get students thinking about the many uses of electricity. Give each student one piece of drawing paper. Ask them to fold it in half. Then fold it into fourths. When the paper is unfolded, there will be four sections. Ask them to draw a picture or write some words (or both) in one of the sections to show the answer to each of these eight questions. (They will need to turn the paper over for the last four questions.)

- How do you use electricity when you fix lunch?
- How do you use electricity when you play a game?
- How do you use electricity when you shop?
- How do you use electricity when you give a party?
- How do you use electricity when you take a shower?
- How do you use electricity when you do your homework?
- How do you use electricity when you get ready for school?
- How do you use electricity when you eat dinner?

SCIENCE  SOUND

SCIENCE AND SIRENS

Ask students: "How many of you have heard a siren? A screech? A thump? A whisper? A knock? Crashes of thunder?" Tell them to think about sounds they have heard. Encourage them to name other sounds. Then ask them to listen to some statements about sound and decide which ones are true and which are false. This will help them ponder how much they know about sound.

- Volume is the loudness or softness of a sound. (true)
- Sounds are caused by vibrations. (true)
- Solid objects cannot vibrate to produce sounds. (false)
- An echo is reflected sound. (true)
- Vocal chords help humans make sound. (true)
- Sound can travel through air. (true)
- Sound cannot travel through liquids. (false)
- It is dangerous for the eardrum to vibrate. (false)
- Sound signals travel to the brain through the optic nerve. (false)
- Some jets can travel faster than the speed of sound. (true)

SCIENCE   GENERAL SCIENCE

GUESS WHAT?

Students often learn better if they use their whole bodies in the process of working with a concept. In this activity, ask students to use their whole bodies (no words or talking) to show a science idea to the class. Give an idea such as one of the following to each student or pair of students. They must silently demonstrate the idea while students try to guess the science object, process, or event.

Examples:

- digestion
- pollution
- Earth's rotation
- sound traveling
- camouflage
- comet circling the Sun
- ocean current
- electricity flowing
- something melting
- something freezing
- rock slide
- glacier moving
- body fighting a germ
- tides
- plant life cycle
- blood circulating
- magnetism
- caterpillar life cycle

SCIENCE   GENERAL SCIENCE

WHERE WOULD YOU FIND IT?

Find out how well students understand a science concept or definition by asking them to place things within their correct context. Name each of the items below. Ask students to give a short description of where the object would be found.
(**Example:** "Where would you find an anemone?"
    Possible answer: "In the ocean.")

Where would you find a . . .

- fossil?
- cerebellum?
- meteorite?
- gill?
- iris?
- molecule?
- molar?
- squid?
- geyser?
- cactus?
- patella?
- galaxy?
- crust?
- electron?
- vibration?
- lava flow?
- trachea?
- supernova?
- fault?
- scale?

SELF-AWARENESS
SELF-AWARENESS
SELF-AWARENESS
SELF-AWARENESS
SELF-AWARENESS
SELF-AWARENESS
SELF-AWARENESS
SELF-AWARENESS
SELF-AWARENESS
SELF-AWARENESS
SELF-AWARENESS

SELF-AWARENESS   SELF-DISCOVERY

FLY ME!

Let each student write a self-description or a list of favorite things on a piece of paper. Ask the students not to sign their names on the paper.

Then let each student form a paper airplane from the paper and instruct them to fly their airplanes across the room.

Each student may pick up one airplane, read the list aloud, and try to identify the writer.

SELF-AWARENESS   MAKING CHOICES

WHICH SIDE?

Give restless students an opportunity to move around and make some choices at the same time.

Have all the students move to one side of the room. Then tell them that they must choose only one of the two things you announce. All students choosing the same thing move to one side of the room. All others move to the other side of the room. Then announce two more things to choose from and let them move accordingly.

    candy bar or ice cream   horse or motorbike
    pencil or paper   hamster or parakeet
    movie or video game   chess set or checker game
    swimming pool or boat   hamburger or pizza

SELF-AWARENESS   SOCIAL RELATIONSHIPS

HIDDEN FRIENDS

Ask students: "How does it make you feel when someone does something nice for you? What kinds of things can you do for someone else that don't cost money or take much time? What things do you like other people to do for you?"

Let students write their names on slips of paper and pass them to you. Then let everyone draw out one slip, making sure that no one gets his or her own name.

Explain that in the next day or so you would like each person to try to do some simple "nice thing" for the person whose name was drawn. The deed should be done without mention of the fact that the student drew that name. Two days later discuss what was done and the feelings that resulted.

SELF-AWARENESS   POSITIVE SELF-IMAGE

I CAN! I CAN!

Are you tired of hearing your students say that they "can't" do something you ask? Provide each of them an opportunity to say, "I can!"

Go around the room quickly, letting one student at a time tell something he or she can do. It doesn't have to be something earth-shaking—just making a positive statement about their abilities will be earth-shaking enough for some students. Being positive can be as habit-forming as being negative. Try to repeat this activity at least once every two or three weeks during the school year.

 SELF-AWARENESS  SELF-IMAGE

ONLY ME

Encourage each student in your class to explore his or her own uniqueness. Have students stand, one at a time, and tell one thing about him- or herself that is unique.

Set the tone for an accepting atmosphere in which each student can feel comfortable sharing personal information.

Examples of "unique" traits:

>I have seven sisters and brothers.
>My eyes are two different colors.
>I broke my leg last week.

 SELF-AWARENESS  SOCIAL RELATIONSHIPS

COMPLIMENT CHAIN

Form a human compliment chain! It helps young people learn to give compliments and learn to accept compliments graciously.

Have the first student turn to the next student and pay him or her a sincere compliment. The complimented student should say "thank you" and then turn to the next student and compliment him or her. Continue the chain until the last student has complimented the first student.

An independent project that is a good follow-up to this is to have students write several compliments for one person on paper strips and form a paper compliment chain from the strips. The chain could be given to the person about whom the compliments were written.

 SELF-AWARENESS  COMMON ATTRIBUTES

JUST LIKE ME

Select two students to stand in front of the room. Each student then selects another student to stand by his or her side and tells one way in which that student is just like him- or herself. Continue taking turns until no students remain to be called, or until one of the students cannot find another student that is like him or her in some way. Be sure to discuss the likenesses as attributes that they share.

Another version would be to have only one student come to the front of the room. That student selects a classmate that is "just like me" in some way. Then the second student calls on a student to compare to and so on.

 SELF-AWARENESS  OBSERVATION

SHOE BUSINESS

How observant are your students? Do they really notice each other? Find out with this activity (best for a time when students are restless and need a little fun). Have everyone stand where they can see each other for one minute. Then have everyone take off their shoes and place them in front of the class (be sure to keep pairs together).

Hold up one pair at a time and see if someone other than the owner can match them with the correct student.

Promise to repeat the activity sometime next week. Watch students keep an eye on each other's feet!

SELF-AWARENESS   GET-ACQUAINTED ACTIVITY

ONE MINUTE TO GO

This is a great "get to know me" activity to do during the first few weeks of school.

Bring one student to the front of the room. Let that student talk about himself or herself for one minute. Ask the student to include information about family, hobbies, likes and dislikes, etc.

Repeat with three or four other students each day. Let the whole class become acquainted with each other in just two weeks. Don't forget to include yourself!

SELF-AWARENESS   SELF-DISCOVERY

I USED TO BE . . .

Students of all ages love to tell tales about what they were like when they were little. (This is even true of 5 and 6-year olds!)

Challenge your students to think about how they have changed throughout their lives so far. Ask them to finish this pair of sentences 4 or 5 times, telling something different each time. They can write or say the sentences. (Note: the words **be** and **am** in the sentences can be modified to fit the topic.)

I used to be . . . . But now I am . . .

Examples:
- I used to be shy. But now I am bold.
- I used to be afraid of monsters. But now I am afraid of dogs.
- I used to fall off my tricycle. But now I ride a two-wheeler.
- I used to hate boys. But now I only hate them a little.
- I used to have just a few freckles. But now I have a thousand freckles.

INDEX

MATH
Counting, 16, 22, 30
Creative thinking, 23
Digits, 18
Finding mistakes, 15
Fractions, 10
Geometry, 11, 21
Guessing numbers, 19
Knowledge, 19
Measurement, 14, 21, 26, 28
Mental math, 10
Mistakes, 15
Numbers, 11, 20, 24
Ordering, 16, 24
Ordinals, 13
Patterns, 12
Place value, 13, 22
Probability, 12
Problem-solving, 17, 20, 23, 25, 27, 29, 30
Real-life situations, 14
Shapes, 21
Size awareness, 28
Story problems, 18, 29
Symbols, 15
Telling time, 17
Time, 17, 26
Units of measure, 26

SOCIAL STUDIES
Advertising, 44
Barter, 47
Cardinal directions, 50
Communities, 40
Community services, 32
Community signs, 41
Consumer responsibilities, 41
Creative thinking, 42
Culture, 47, 48
Currency, 35
Directions, 50
Economics, 39, 41, 42, 43, 44, 45, 48, 49, 50
Famous persons, 34
Geography, 33, 36, 38, 45
Globe skills, 35
History, 46, 49
Jobs, 37, 39
Laws, 43
Manufacturing, 49, 50
Map skills, 34, 35, 50
Money, 36, 37, 38
Opportunity cost, 43
Polling, 46
Pricing, 38
Private property, 40
Property, 40
Public property, 40
Rules and laws, 43
Service jobs, 39
Social groups, 33
Symbols, 48
Time sequence, 32
Time lines, 32
Traditions, 47

LANGUAGE ARTS
Alliteration, 67
Analogies, 59
Categorizing, 69
Cause and effect, 71
Coining words, 65
Communication, 58, 66
Context, 58
Creative thinking, 70
Descriptive language, 57
Dictionary skills, 69
Facts and opinions, 64
General knowledge, 70
Homonyms, 57
Idioms, 52
Impromptu speaking, 54
Irregular plurals, 72
Listening, 62
Past tenses, 53
Plurals, 72
Poetry, 60
Reference skills, 63
Related words, 61
Self-Expression, 65, 71
Sentences, 54
Speaking, 54
Syllables, 56
Synonyms, 54
Table of Contents, 68
Tenses, 53
Textbook information, 53
Topic selection, 56
Verbs, 53
Word play, 66
Words, 55, 57, 60, 61, 62, 63, 65, 67, 68, 72
Writing, 59, 64

SCIENCE
Animal movements, 79
Body, human, 82, 83
Bones, 83
Cause and effect, 76
Classification, 77
Diseases and disorders, 83
Electricity, 87
Energy, 85
Fields of science, 74, 85
Floating, 85
Form and function, 76
General science, 88
Habitats, 79
History of science, 74, 75
Life, 78
Matter, 84
Measurement, 86
Observation, 77
Oceans, 80
Science,
    applications, 75
    Earth, 80
    fields, 74, 85
    general, 88
    history, 74, 75
    space, 81
Senses, 82
Solar system, 81
Sound, 87
Water, 85
Weather, 86

SELF-AWARENESS
Common attributes, 93
Get-Acquainted, 94
Making choices, 90
Observation, 93
Self-discovery, 90, 94
Self-image, 91, 92
Social relationships, 91, 92